The soul; or, An inquiry into Scriptural psychology, as developed by the use of the terms, soul, spi

George Bush

Copyright © BiblioLife, LLC

This book represents a historical reproduction of a work originally published before 1923 that is part of a unique project which provides opportunities for readers, educators and researchers by bringing hard-to-find original publications back into print at reasonable prices. Because this and other works are culturally important, we have made them available as part of our commitment to protecting, preserving and promoting the world's literature. These books are in the "public domain" and were digitized and made available in cooperation with libraries, archives, and open source initiatives around the world dedicated to this important mission.

We believe that when we undertake the difficult task of re-creating these works as attractive, readable and affordable books, we further the goal of sharing these works with a global audience, and preserving a vanishing wealth of human knowledge.

Many historical books were originally published in small fonts, which can make them very difficult to read. Accordingly, in order to improve the reading experience of these books, we have created "enlarged print" versions of our books. Because of font size variation in the original books, some of these may not technically qualify as "large print" books, as that term is generally defined; however, we believe these versions provide an overall improved reading experience for many.

THE SOUL;

OR,

AN INQUIRY INTO SCRIPTURAL PSYCHOLOGY,

AS DEVELOPED BY

THE USE OF THE TERMS, SOUL, SPIRIT, LIFE, ETC.,

VIEWED IN ITS BEARINGS ON

THE DOCTRINE OF THE RESURRECTION.

By GEORGE BUSH,

PROFESSOR OF HEBREW IN THE NEW YORK CITY UNIVERSITY.

NEW-YORK.
J. S. REDFIELD, CLINTON HALL.
1845.

ENTERED, according to Act of Congress, in the year 1845, by
GEORGE BUSH,
In the Clerk's Office of the District Court for the Southern District of
New-York.

J. F. TROW & CO., PRINTERS,
33 Ann-street.

PREFACE.

THE present work has grown, by a very natural sequence, out of the farther investigations to which I have been prompted by the tenor of several elaborate critiques on the volume recently given to the world under the title of "Anastasis," or the Resurrection of the Body considered So far as that work could be considered as propounding a distinct theory of the Resurrection, it is that of a *spiritual*, or rather *psychical*, body developed, by a natural law, from the material body at death. To establish this position is the drift of that portion of the volume embraced under the head of "The Rational Argument" The position itself, if founded on a solid basis, obviously strikes at the root of the prevalent notions on the general subject; for if a spiritual body be actually assumed by every individual upon his abandonment of the material body, there is plainly a very troublesome incongruity in the idea of the soul's receiving still another spiritual body at what is called the last day, or the era of the final consummation. Accordingly it is upon this part of the argument that the main force of the rebutting criticism has spent itself The reviewers, as by common consent, have selected this as the one grand point of assault, and aimed to show that there was an entire lack of proof of the existence of any such psychical element in our being which, as a *tertium quid* between the spirit and the gross material body, could be regarded in any sense as a *vehiculum animæ*, or ethereal corporeity for the inner intellectual and moral principle which forms the *ipseity*, *selfhood*, or *essential hypostasis* of the man

This line of argument urged, as it has been, with great vehemence from several quarters, has naturally led to a fuller examination of the grounds on which the offending theory was originally propounded. In the work itself it was put forth as an alternative theory; that is to say as the necessary result of a chain of reasoning which, if sound, went to set aside the established belief of the reconstruction in some sense, of the perished body tenanted by the soul during its earthly life. As there is clearly to be a resurrection after death—as *something* must rise and live again in another world—and as I have assumed to show that that something is *not* the body which is deposited in the grave —I was obviously called upon to designate affirmatively *what it is*. This I have stated to be a *psychical body* eliminated at death from the material body, the *essential nature* of which, however, I do not hold it incumbent upon me to define, inasmuch as all parties are alike ignorant of the ontological attributes of the *psyche* (ψυχὴ), which at the same time all parties alike acknowledge to exist. The extent of my position is, that the psychical body, *whatever be its essential nature*, is assumed at death, and not at some indefinitely future period. In support of this hypothesis I relied rather upon physiological and psychological considerations, than upon the direct testimony of Scripture.

In consequence, however, of the stern arraignment, at the bar of the pulpit and the press, of the view propounded, I have been led to a closer investigation of its merits as submitted to the test of Scripture, and in the ensuing pages have planted my defence of it not solely upon a rational but upon a strictly exegetical basis. What was before *suggested* is here *affirmed*. I claim to have shown, by a rigid and unimpeachable process of interpretation, that the inspired oracles unequivocally recognize the tripartite distinction of man's nature into *spirit, soul,* and *body*—that when the body is forsaken at death the *spiritual* and the *psychical* elements survive in coexistence together and constitute the *true man*, which in actual usage is commonly designated by the single term *soul*—that inasmuch as the *psychical* principle, even in the present life, is the true seat and subject of what are commonly called *bodily sensations*, this principle is legitimately to be regarded as performing the same office for the *spirit* in the other life; or in other words, that the *soul* necessarily involves the idea conveyed by the phrase *spiritual body*—and, finally, that the fact of the immediate possession of such a body after death precludes the hypothesis of the investiture of the spirit at any future period, with any *other* corporeity derived from the relics, however formed or fashioned, of the present material body. These are the points which I profess to establish by the course of reasoning pursued in the present essay. The soundness of the conclusions must evidently depend upon the soundess of the premises. If I have given a wrong interpretation of the language of Scripture, it can doubtless be shown by confronting it with the right; and I must be allowed to demand that whoever assumes the work of refutation he shall not content himself with a bare negation of results, and especially that he shall not think to overwhelm the argument by the violent outcry of *Rationalism, Neologism*, or *Infidelity*, as characterizing the principles of exegesis which bring out these results. It is simply a question of sound or unsound interpretation, and I do not hesitate to affirm that even on the supposition that I may have erred in my exegesis, there is still so much of plausibility and probability in the senses assigned to the inspired language, that it is impossible for any one justly to maintain that an honest and truth-loving mind could not have adopted them without giving occasion for doubt as to the *moral state* of the inner man in so doing. And yet what but the *moral character* of a false interpretation can render it a fit subject of rebuke and reprobation ? And from what is its *moral character* derived but from the *moral state* of its author, especially when his opinions concern a fundamental doctrine of Revelation ? There are doubtless some very nice questions to be settled under this head. We are constrained to believe that there is nothing that can justify a severe denunciation of the canons of exegesis which conduct to conclusions at variance with established belief upon important doctrines of religion, but the *virtual* assumption that a certain moral posture of the mind will not fail to see revealed truth in a certain light, and the fact of its not being seen in this light is *prima facie* evidence that that condition is wanting. This rule of judgment, it is true, is seldom distinctly asserted. But we see not but it must be inwardly held and acted upon in order to warrant the hard measure which is often dealt out to so-styled errant opinions. At any rate, if the soundness of the principle is not actually recognized, that *a book is a fair exponent of the man*, it would seem that there was a just requisition for the avowal of *some* principle under the tutelage of which the stern procedure above alluded to towards the propagators of alleged intellectual errors should be vindicated. Meanwhile I venture for myself to continue a straightforward course of biblical inquiry, and to give to the world, under the general prompting of such motives as seem to me to become a Christian, the conclusions at which I arrive from the evidence that forces itself upon my mind. If valid, they will probably approve themselves to those who may think them worthy their attention. If fallacious, the exposure of the error is but the penalty that every sensible man is prepared to pay for the possibility of error in the free expression of his opinions.

G. B.

New-York, August, 1845.

CONTENTS

	Page.
PRELIMINARY REMARKS, ...	9
CHAP. I. Scriptural Distinction between Soul and Body, .	20
CHAP. II. Import of Original Scriptural Terms for Soul, .	23
§ 1. נֶפֶשׁ (*nephesh*), ψυχή (*psuche*), Anima, Soul, Life, ...	23
§ 2. נֶפֶשׁ in the sense of Living Creature with the uniform Accompaniment of חַיָּה, . .	28
§ 3. נֶפֶשׁ in the sense of Life, ψυχή, Anima, the Vital Principle by which the Body lives, .	30
§ 4. נֶפֶשׁ as the Seat of Sensation, the Subject of Bodily Appetites, Desires, and the various kinds of Sensual or Animal Affections, .	33
§ 5. נֶפֶשׁ in the sense of Animus, Rational Soul, Mind, and considered as the Seat of various Passions, Emotions, the Affections pertaining to a Rational Being, such as Love, Joy, Fear, Sorrow, Hope, Hatred, Revenge, Contempt, &c., ...	41
§ 6. נֶפֶשׁ in the sense of Person, . .	46
§ 7. נֶפֶשׁ in the sense of One's Self, or the interior and ground element of his being, the Personal Hypostasis, ...	56
§ 8. נֶפֶשׁ in the sense of Dead Body, .	62
CHAP. III. Import of Original Scriptural Terms for Spirit, .	65
§ 1. רוּחַ (*ruahh*), πνεῦμα (*pneuma*), Spirit, .	65
§ 2. רוּחַ in the sense of Breath, . .	67
§ 3. רוּחַ in the sense of Wind, Ἄνεμος, .	69

CONTENTS.

§ 4. רוּחַ in the sense of Anima, ψυχή, Animal Life, Vital Spirit, or the Principle of Life as embodied and manifested in the Breath of the Mouth and Nostrils, . . . 71

§ 5. רוּחַ in the sense of Animus, πνεῦμα, Spirit, the Mind, viewed as the Seat and Subject of Thought, but more especially of Emotion, Feeling, Passion, and Affection, . 73

§ 6. רוּחַ in the sense of a Spirit, a Personal Agent, whether good or bad, whether spoken of Angels, Demons, or Men, . . . 84

CHAP. IV. נְשָׁמָה (neshâmâh), πνοή (pnoē), Breath, Spirit, . 98
§ 1 נְשָׁמָה in the sense of Breath, . . . 98
§ 2. נְשָׁמָה in the sense of Mind, the Intelligent Principle, ... 99

CHAP. V. לֵב (lēb), καρδία (kardia), Heart, . . . 100
§ 1. לֵב in the sense of Heart as a Physical Organ of the Body, ... 101
§ 2. לֵב in the sense of Mind, Understanding, Wisdom, the Faculty of Thinking, &c, . 103
§ 3. לֵב as denoting the Principle which is the Seat and Subject of Sensations, Feelings, Emotions, and Passions of various kinds, as Love, Joy, Confidence, Hope, Hatred, Contempt, Sorrow, Despair, &c., . . 105

CHAP. VI. General Results, ... 107

APPENDIX. Conflicting Views of the Resurrection, . . 133

THE SOUL.

Preliminary Remarks.

ANTHROPOLOGY is the appropriated term for *the science of man.* Its two grand divisions, founded upon the twofold distinction of man's nature, are *physiology* and *psychology,* the first relating to the body, the second to the soul Man, in both these departments, is a proper theme of scientific research. The phenomena of his being, the laws of his animal and intellectual economy, constitute a field of inquiry which lies open to the freest investigation. The exhibitions of divine power and wisdom and benignity which shine forth in the human frame draw largely upon our devout admiration, and are among the thousand-fold works of the Almighty Architect which are diligently "sought out of all them that have pleasure therein." Man is a microcosm involving a miniature universe of wonders, the complete development of which is the work of ages. It is possible, however, to certify the results of our inquiries in this department to a given point, and when this point is attained, whatever it be, it is impossible to say that we may not advance beyond it to another, and thence to another still, and so on indefinitely, in continual approximation to a perfect knowledge of the structure of our bodies and our souls. The presumption is not in saying, "Thus far have we come," but in saying, "Thus far shalt thou go and no farther;" for it is not in the compass of human intelligence to set limits to the possible extent of acquisition in our knowledge of any and every part of God's works As the field is boundless, so the progress in it is interminable. Nor does the fact of a Revelation having been accorded us put any bar in the way of our profoundest inquest, on the ground of Reason, into the great truths which form its themes. The nature, state, and destiny of man enter largely into the disclosures of holy writ; but why should this prevent the prosecution of our researches, by the independent lights which God has given us, into the internal constitution of the bodies and souls of which we find ourselves possessed? Is there any danger that we shall by and by reach a point where Reason and Revelation will come into inevitable conflict? How can this be, if Reason and Revelation acknowledge the same divine source? Is not the universe itself a Revelation of its Author,—a Revelation made to the Reason of intelligent beings,—and is it conceivable that the disclosures it contains should be in any way at variance with the *sense* of a written record announcing a portion of the very truths which the universe comprises? We are far, indeed, from affirming that unassisted Reason can grasp *all* the verities which may be supposed to enter into a Revelation from God. But so far as Revelation and Reason cover a common ground, the last inductions of the one must necessarily harmonize with the true-meant averments of the other; and the only question that can arise is as to the *certainty* of the results of the latter, and the *true interpretation* of the former.

There are doubtless cases where the apparently irresistible conclusions of science do conflict with the apparently obvious sense of Scripture, so that there seems no alternative but that the one must give way before the more imperative claims of the other. The results of Astronomical and Geological science present a case in point. Now what shall be done in an emergency like this? The evidence of the truth in both these departments is so absolutely decisive and overwhelming, that the mind which appreciates it feels that it would be guilty of doing a moral violence to its higher

PRELIMINARY REMARKS. 11

instincts to reject it, and one upon which God himself would frown. And this conviction, be it observed, often bears down in all its force upon minds penetrated with the deepest reverence for the inspired volume, and who would not hesitate a moment to discard their clearest rational deductions were they inwardly assured, beyond the possibility of a doubt, that the *verity of the sense* of Revelation perfectly agreed with the *import of the letter*. But here they are compelled to pause. Here they are met by certain questions which it is impossible for them to put away. They cannot avoid an inquiry into the *principles* on which a divine Revelation is to be interpreted, and these principles, they are convinced, must be determined by the leading *scope* and *design* with which such a Revelation is given to the world. Is that *design* such as, in its own nature, will consist with a presentation of natural and scientific phenomena in the language, not always of absolute truth, but of common, popular, and prevailing apprehension? We see not how it can reasonably be questioned, that the scope of the sacred volume is predominantly *moral* and not *scientific*. It does not *profess*, therefore, to lay open the veritable *nature of things* in those departments which the human mind may explore by the lighted candle of its own intelligence. Speaking in order to be understood, it speaks as it could be and would be understood. It takes a multitude of things as facts, because they were then regarded as facts, and yet all along makes a tacit allowance for the rectifying results of deeper insight and wider discovery. If then in the progress of inquiry we reach such results, why shall we not abide by them? And what disparagement is cast upon Revelation if, holding its oracles sacred in the *moral* sphere which it professes to occupy, we still make the *ascertained facts* of science and philosophy the criterion by which its *true sense* on those subjects is to be determined? All the appointments of God are honored in proportion as they are regarded in reference to their *true end and design*. If they are deflected, in our application of them, from their controlling purpose, we honor them no more than if we neglected them altogether. We repeat then that no contemptuous disrespect of Revelation is chargeable upon the man of science when he obeys the laws of sound reason in adhering to conclusions forced upon him by the incontestable *facts* of any field of research. Are the asserted facts real facts? This is the only question. If they are, it is impossible they should be contravened by the *sense* of Scripture, whatever may be made of the *letter*.

This train of remark applies in all its force to the subject of our present investigation. We believe it is possible to come, through the use of appropriate media, to such a knowledge of the physical and psychical constitution of man, as shall actually force upon us certain conclusions as to the conditions of his future being which cannot be resisted. But the page of inspiration deals expressly with the destiny of man in another life, and it cannot be questioned, that the *letter* of its statements does in some instances convey a meaning to the mind which is at variance with what we firmly believe to be the *absolute truth* on this head. Guided by the sense which floats, as it were, on the surface of Scripture, we should no doubt most naturally receive the impression, that that part of our compound being which we call *the soul*, went forth at death in a purely disembodied state, and so remained for an indefinite tract of ages, till at the period denominated *the last day—the day of judgment—the day of the resurrection—the day of Christ's second advent—the final consummation, including the physical catastrophe of the globe*—the perished body should again be raised, and the long exiled soul again restored to its former tenement, thenceforth to sojourn in it forever. Now we are for ourselves fully persuaded that every item in this scheme of Eschatology is utterly erroneous, baseless, and delusive. In regard to most of them we believe that they are even directly at war with the most fair and legitimate teaching of the *letter* of the sacred record, and those which are not, are irreconcilably contrary to its *genuine sense.* On the one hand, we confidently deny, that a sound philological exegesis can adduce any satisfactory evidence of such a revealed event as is popularly understood by the "end of the world," implying its physical conflagration or termination in any way whatever. The attempt to do this will inevitably bring the predictions of Isaiah, Ezekiel, Daniel, John, and our Lord himself, into such fatal collision, that the authority of one or the other is effectually annulled. They cannot all stand without standing in direct antagonism with each other. Upon this ground alone, if there were no other, we should be prepared to deny that the common views of the Resurrection could be correct. *There is no place for it at the end of the world, because there is no end of the world revealed.*

On the other hand, we are equally firm in the belief, that the scientific survey of man, considered physiologically and psychologically, brings us irresistibly to the inference, that whatever be the true mode of his existence after death, it is entered upon at once, and that the idea of the future reunion of these constituent elements of his being is entirely gratuitous and nugatory. The grounds of this induction, however, it is not our present purpose to recite at length. Assuming it for granted—what no one will deny—that man, during his life, is made up of body and soul, and that at death his body remains behind and turns to corruption, while his soul issues forth undying into the world of spirits, the facts of the case, sustained by the analogies of nature, would inevitably lead to the inference, that the body would never live again in connexion with the soul, were it not for the *apprehended import* of Revelation, which is usually understood to assert such a future resuscitation and reunion. As we believe this natural inference to be the *true one*, notwithstanding the apparent contrary teaching of Scripture, our object in what follows in the present essay will be to show, that there is nothing in the language of the sacred writers in respect to the *soul, spirit, mind,* or whatever the immaterial and immortal part of man may be termed, which, *rightly interpreted*, conflicts with this view, or which soundly favors the belief, on this subject, that has become established in the current theology of Christendom.

But it will naturally be asked how the belief became so generally established, and how has it so long held its ground, if there really be no adequate support for it in the word of Inspiration? The solution, we conceive, is to be sought in the fact, that the phraseology employed by Christ and the apostles is drawn, for the most part, *from the phenomena of life and death as they strike the outward senses, and have relation to the body.* It is the body alone which comes under the cognizance of the senses. A living man is, in ordinary parlance, a man living in a body. A dead man is a man whose body has become defunct. The necessities of language enforce this mode of speech more or less in all ages, and in the face of higher knowledge; still more unavoidable was it in the circumstances under which the Scriptural revelation was imparted to the world. The great truth to be given out was, that *man*, in the true reality of his manhood, was to live again. In what that manhood essentially consisted might not then be adequately known. The lapse of the ages would pour all requisite light upon it. In the mean time the divine teachers, under the guidance of the Spirit of Truth would not content themselves simply with declaring that the *soul* should survive the dissolution of the body, for although the term *soul* actually implies, in sacred usage, all that constitutes the essential *person*, yet their hearers might have been so far influenced by the subtleties of the philosophers as to have understood by it, in the vaguest sense, a mere thinking principle, a bare intelligent breath, exhaled into the infinite ether, of which it was deemed little else than a component part. This would be an utterly inadequate view of the truth. It is in fact the *man*, in the full integrity of his being and attributes, that is translated into the world unseen, as we shall hope more clearly to evince in the sequel. And with a view to the fuller intimation of this fact, our Saviour, especially, employs a language which, naturally though not necessarily involving corporeal ideas, would elevate their minds to a more fitting conception of the grand reality.

The train of reasoning by which the non-resurrection of the material body is attempted to be made out we have presented in another volume. This it is not our purpose here to recapitulate. We remain unshaken in the conviction that the common doctrine of the resurrection is alike abhorrent to Revelation and to Reason. We fully believe that, *from the necessity of the case*, man enters upon his resurrection-state at death, and our present aim is to evince, that nothing can be inferred from the *usus loquendi* of the sacred writers in regard to the word *soul* or *spirit*, adverse to this view.

It will be seen, however, that our argument is rather of a *negative* than a *positive* character. We do not assume to disclose affirmatively the precise nature of the spiritual body which is developed at death from the natural body. The extent of our positions is, that that body, *whatever be its nature*, is assumed when the material body is abandoned; and with a view to this result we endeavor to show, that the term *soul*, in its legitimate usage, involves the idea of a *spiritual body*. Still we deem ourselves left uninstructed from this source in regard to the *absolute verity*. The Scriptures do not speak *philosophically* on the subject—they do not profess to make us acquainted with the *intrinsic nature* of the ground-element of human existence. They simply recognize the fact that man is a compound being, corporeal and intellectual, and predicate certain attributes of the one part or the other, according as their particular scope required, and the existence of which the universal consciousness of men would at once assure to them. The possession of a soul and a body, severally distinguished by peculiar properties, is a matter of consciousness and not of reasoning, and the grand purposes of a divine Revelation, require no scientific exposition of the elementary structure of the being to whom it is addressed. In the department of inquiry which we here enter, we must hold, that the conclusions which we should naturally draw from the obvious phenomena of life and death, are to stand good until it can be clearly shown that they are countervailed by opposing evidence, too strong to be resisted, that they are not sound. The issue, therefore, is joined upon the comparative claims of the inductions of Reason and of the *letter* of Revelation to govern our belief in regard to the verity of things in the field of physiology and pneumatology. For ourselves, we contend that as the human mind is constituted it will and it must abide by the conclusions which it reaches from the evidence of the facts before it. The main facts with which the present discussion has to do, are the facts relating to the connexion of the soul with its material dwelling place, the body. Taking for granted the perpetual flux of the particles which in this life compose our bodies, and their transition after death into innumerable other forms of organized existence, we affirm that their future recomposition into the *same* bodies, to be inhabited by the *same* souls, does so much violence to the laws of human belief, that we are perfectly warranted in subjecting to the most rigid ordeal of interpretation those divine announcements which *seem* to warrant such a conclusion. Nor do we shrink from following out this principle to the utmost extent of its applicability to every asserted fact and doctrine of Revelation. The principle may be adopted in perfect consistency with the admission, that the compass of Revelation embraces disclosures which transcend the highest oracles of Reason, and which it receives simply on the authority of the Revealer, as incontestably taught by the plain sense of the record, and against which Reason has no voice to utter. They are truths lying out of the bounds of her domain, and which consequently she cannot gainsay, when they come authenticated by the unequivocal declaration of Jehovah himself. Here the office of Reason is simply to apply the established laws of interpretation to certain inspired averments, and when their true sense is elicited, reverently to receive them, however much our intelligence may be tasked adequately to *comprehend* all that may be involved in their import. We receive them because we believe that inspiration means to affirm them, and because, from the nature of the subject, we are unable to adduce from other sources any sufficient grounds for rejecting them.

But the case is wholly different when the enunciations of holy writ respect matters that are not addressed purely to Faith—when, although coming within the sphere of Revelation, they come at the same time within the sphere of our native faculties. On these points Reason speaks and will be heard, and the attempt to stifle its voice is a mistaken mode of honoring Revelation. It is, however, a fair demand on the part of the friends of Revelation, that any alleged deductions of Reason which may appear to conflict with the literal statements of Scripture shall be substantiated by adequate evidence, or evidence that cannot fail to satisfy a calm, reflecting mind on a full view of all the conditions. We do not say it must be of such a nature as shall at once, as soon as stated, immediately command the assent of every intellect to which it is submitted, for there is no doubt that the long established and traditionary sense which has been grafted upon the letter of Scripture does put the mind into an attitude unfavorable to a due estimate of the force of objections urged against that sense. Thus, for instance, in regard to the subject before us, it cannot be questioned that the deep-seated belief that the term *resurrection* denotes the *resurrection of the same body at some indefinitely future period*, presents a strong barrier to the admission of the evidence against this, drawn from the conceded facts of the constant flux of particles during life, and their dissipation and re-formation in other unions after death. Yet we do not hesitate to maintain, that in the view of enlightened reason this fact is of itself so imperative against the belief, that it will give way in every mind that yields to its convictions, and when professedly retained, it will be with a latent distrust, and like a weight that is kept up above the surface of the earth by some force that is able for the present to overcome its gravitating tendency.

But we rely not alone on the evidence drawn from this source.* We contend that the true constitution of man, physiologically and psychologically viewed, forces upon us the conclusion, that what is termed the *spiritual body* has no relation whatever to the *buried remains* of the material body. We deem ourselves prepared to show, that that part of our nature which survives death, and which is termed the *soul*, fully answers to every just idea which we can form of the body of the resurrection. The proof upon this point constitutes the subject-matter of the present volume. It is drawn from a combined view of the clear results of anthropology, and the equally clear characteristics of sacred philology.

It will, however, be readily inferred from the tenor of our preceding remarks, that the object proposed by our inquiry, under the head of *Scriptural Psychology*, cannot be the development of *a true, formal, scientific system of the soul*. It can only be the display of the *actual usage* of the sacred writers in regard to certain terms which recognize as facts certain principles and properties of our internal nature. We do not mean by this, of course, that the ideas conveyed by the terms may not be strictly *true*, as far as their import reaches, but that there is a region of truth lying without and beyond the extent of meaning which, in actual usage, they legitimately bear. In the endeavor, therefore, to compass this ulterior truth relating to the soul, we are not to deem ourselves withheld, by the sense which the Scriptures properly attach to the terms, from the affirmation of any more extended sense of them that may be warranted by adequate evidence. Of the degree to which this evidence exists every one must judge for himself. But for ourselves we believe it to be impossible to establish any results of an exegetical character in regard to the prevailing usage of the terms *soul* and *spirit* that shall at all conflict with that theory of the resurrection which makes it to imply the development of a spiritual body at death. So far, in fact, as the ascertainable sense of the words bears upon the conditions of existence in another world, we hope to show that the evidence decidedly preponderates in favor of the idea, that *the soul is the real man*, and that he begins to live at once after death in the full integrity of his true manhood, and this necessarily implies the possession of a spiritual body. But upon this opinion it will be premature to dwell until we have fully exhibited the usage. Upon this we now enter, proposing to take up the several words in succession, and to present such copious illustrations under each as will serve to establish the soundness of the interpretation given.

CHAPTER I.

The Scriptural Distinction of Soul and Body.

THE distinction in man's nature between the two great elements of *Soul* and *Body* is so obvious and important that it could scarcely fail to be observed and expressed by appropriate terms in the very infancy of the race and of language. Yet it is remarkable that the biblical Hebrew contains no single word answering, in fixed and definite import, to the Greek σῶμα, the Latin *corpus*, or the English *body*. It exhibits eight or ten different terms which are occasionally rendered *body*, but no one of them has that peculiar appropriated sense which we recognize in the corresponding terms in the languages above mentioned. The ordinary distinctive word for *body* in Hebrew is בָּשָׂר *básár, flesh*, the mere obvious material of which the body is composed. The verbal form to which this word is lexically referred, especially as illustrated in its linguistic affinities, seems to convey, in its primary import, the idea of *fairness, beauty,* or perhaps more strictly that of *ruddiness* or *brightness,* particularly as evinced in the countenance, as the effect of *joyful and exhilarating tidings;* whence the verb בִּשֵּׂר *bissēr* is usually rendered *to cheer with glad tidings, to bring or announce good news* to any one. The noun, בָּשָׂר, however, is invariably rendered *flesh,* though quite as frequently perhaps in a metaphorical as in a literal sense, i. e. as equivalent to man's *fallen, sinful, and corrupt nature.* In this sense it is not related to our present object, nor in its literal sense does it require more than a passing allusion, as our grand aim is to investigate the usage that obtains in regard to the terms designating the *soul*. The distinction, however, to which we allude is sometimes expressed by "*flesh* and *spirit,*" and sometimes by "*heart* and *flesh*," which is entirely tantamount. In a few instances the entire man is denominated from the *flesh* as equivalent to the *body*, as he is in other instances from the *soul*. Thus, Gen 2 24, "They shall be *one flesh*." i e one person. Eccl. 2 3, "I sought to give *myself* (Heb. בְּבָשָׂרִי *my flesh*) unto wine" The more subtle distinction, familiar in our philosophy, between substances strictly *material* and *immaterial* appears not to be expressly recognized in the sacred writings. The passage which comes nearest to it is perhaps Is 31. 3, "Their horses are *flesh* and not *spirit*." That such a distinction is, in the nature of things, well founded, there can be no doubt, though it may be of too subtle a nature for our discrimination, when matter is contemplated in its most tenuous forms.* But we find no evidence that such metaphysical nicety entered into the conceptions of the inspired penmen of the Scriptures.

At the same time we think the remark not superfluous, that in regard to this, as well as many other subjects treated in the sacred volume, a discrimination is to be made between the true-meant and deep-laid sense of the Holy Spirit and the conscious personal sense of the writers in inditing the language employed. Acting as mere amanuenses of the Divine Dictator of the word, nothing is more easily conceivable, than that the meaning which their mind affixed to a multitude of words may have been vastly transcended by the more fundamental import flowing from the depth of the

---

* "We really know not wherein the elements of matter consist and although we are acquainted with some of its properties, we do not know its *essence;* neither are we sure that it may not possess properties, or assume forms, with which we are unacquainted, and which are too subtle to be recognized by our senses Hence we do not consider the question of the materiality of the soul as being very *important*, because what we call *sp i tual, may*, in fact, be an infinitely fine modification of matter, far too subtle to be apprehended by our present powers" *Newnham on Reciprocal Influence of Body and Mind,* p 97.

infinite intelligence, which must of course be regarded as compassing all the absolute verities involved in the nature of the themes. It does not seem to be at all necessary to a sound view of inspiration that the sacred writers should have truly understood all the truth which they were commissioned to indite, or in other words, that their sense of the terms they employed should be deemed the measure of the sense of the Holy Ghost. Accordingly, as the absolute truth of the subject matters of the word becomes in time more fully developed by the light of science or the course of providence, we may find that the terms made use of do actually interpret themselves more in accordance with the essential and philosophical verity of things than we can suppose possible of the same words when limited to the narrower sense of the human scribes by whose hands they were penned.— This principle must certainly be admitted in regard to a large portion of the prophetic Scriptures, and we see no reason to question its applicability to the department we are now considering. As the true constitution of man mentally and corporeally becomes more fully unfolded by the progress of physiology and psychology, we cannot doubt that the language of revelation will yield, in great measure, a meaning which, without violence, shall strikingly conform to the actual results of discovery and deduction in this field of inquiry. The justness, however, of this suggestion will probably disclose itself more fully in the process and the close of the philological researches which we have proposed to ourselves, and upon which we enter in a careful investigation of the import of the word *soul* in its various Scriptural relations.

CHAPTER II.

Import of Original Scriptural Terms for Soul.

§ 1.

נֶפֶשׁ *(nephesh)*, ψυχή *(psuche), Anima, Soul, Life.*

The current rendering of this term in our English version is *soul* But this does not strictly define the word, as *soul* is very variously used, and the true idea is to be elicited, if at all, from a critical inquest into the genuine purport of its Hebrew original. Lexicography assumes it as a normal derivative from the radical נָפַשׁ *náphash, to breathe, to respire,* with which coincide the cognates נָשַׁף *náshaph,* נָשַׁב *náshav,* נָשַׁם *násham*, and שָׁאַף *sháaph,* all of them having the import of *breathing* or *blowing*, or in some way conveying the idea of *air in motion* The word נֶפֶשׁ, however, is not found in Kal, or the simplest verbal form, but only in Niphal, or the passive in the sense of *taking breath*, or *being refreshed*, especially after fatigue The word in this form occurs only in the three following instances.

Ex. 23 12, "That the stranger *may be refreshed* (יִנָּפֵשׁ. Gr. ἀναψύξῃ) "

" 31. 17, "And on the seventh day he rested and *was refreshed* (וַיִּנָּפַשׁ. Gr. ἐπαύσατο)."

2 Sam. 16. 14, " And the king, and all the people that were with him, came weary, *and refreshed themselves there* (וַיִּנָּפֵשׁ שָׁם. Gr. ἀνεψύξαν ἐκεῖ) "

The relation between the words is indeed as obvious as that in English between *breathe* and *breath*, yet there is every probability that the verb יִנָּפֵשׁ is a mere denominative formed from the noun נֶפֶשׁ, instead of the reverse of the process being the fact. This is according to a very prevalent analogy in Hebrew, of which copious examples are given in the Grammars of Gesenius and Ewald. Thus we find זָכַר *to be born a male,* from זָכָר *a male;* דִּשֵּׁן *to remove ashes,* from דֶּשֶׁן *ashes;* הֶעֱרֵל *to show oneself uncircumcised,* from עָרְלָה *foreskin.* The noun, therefore, we think, is to be regarded as primitive, unless, as Gesenius suggests, it may be formed by transposition of letters from נָשַׁב *to breathe, to blow.* However this may be, it is not to be questioned that the radical import of the word is *breath, as a visible indication of life,* in consequence of which the two senses of the word, *breath* and *life,* in actual usage, very frequently run into each other, as will be evident from the citations which follow. So far then as *soul* stands as a correct representative of נֶפֶשׁ it imports in the main the *principle of animal life, the vital spirit,* as manifested by the *breath,* but not necessarily including the idea of *intellectual faculties,* which though occasionally implied in the use of the term in certain connections, is still entirely adventitious to the primitive sense.

The corresponding Greek term ψυχή comes from ψύχω, of which the primary sense is held by lexicographers to be *to breathe, to blow,* and thence *to render cold, to be cool,* as an effect of breathing or blowing upon one; and hence by natural transition *to refresh.* From the primitive sense comes ψυχή, *soul,* and from the secondary ψυχός, *cold.* The dominant import of ψυχή is undoubtedly *life* as indicated by the act of *breathing,* which is the principal visible distinction between a *living* and a *dead* animal, and this import it evidently has in numerous instances in which it is translated *soul,* as will be seen from the citations soon to be given. Yet nothing is clearer than that in this sense ψυχή is broadly distinguished from another Greek term ζωή, which is also rendered by the same English word *life,* and which is uniformly employed in all such phrases as—" enter into *life*"— " see *life*"—" inherit eternal *life*"—" have eternal *life*" —" pass from death unto *life*"—" endure unto everlasting *life*"—" light of *life*"—" word of *life*"—" bread of *life*"—" resurrection of *life*," &c. In these instances it obviously denotes a higher, more spiritual, more transcendental principle than is indicated by the word ψυχή, which is more strictly applicable to the principle of *vitality as connected with animal organization*. In John, 12. 25, we meet with both terms in close connection: "He that hateth his *life* (ψυχήν) in this world, shall keep it unto *life* (ζωήν) eternal." It would be entirely contrary to prevailing analogy to have used ψυχήν in both these clauses. Yet there are a few sporadic cases in which ζωή occurs in the lower sense of mere physical life. Thus, Luke 1. 75, "In holiness and righteousness before him, all the days of our *life* (ζωῆς.)" Luke, 16. 25, "Son, remember that thou in thy *lifetime* (ζωῇ) receivedst thy good things." Acts, 8. 33, "Who shall declare his generation? for his *life* (ζωή) is taken from the earth." Acts, 17. 25, "Seeing he giveth to all *life* (ζωήν), and breath, and all things." Rom 8 38, "For I am persuaded that neither death, nor *life* (ζωή), nor angels, nor principalities, &c, shall be able to separate us from the love of God." Comp. 1 Cor. 3 22. 1 Cor. 15. 19, "If in this *life* (ζωῇ) only we have hope in Christ, we are of all men most miserable." Heb 7 3, "Having neither beginning of days nor end of *life* (ζωῆς)." Comp. v. 16. These are all the cases, out of one hundred and thirty two, in which the word occurs in this sense in the New Testament. In the Septuagint it is never employed as a rendering of נפש, but almost uniformly of חיים *life* or *living*. In its true interior sense it conveys the idea of *good, enjoyment, happiness*, in connection with that of *life*, and the import of *duration* is plainly accessory, as it is natural to conceive of that which is *living*, and as such *enjoying*, as at the same time *enduring*, though the ideas are intrinsically separable. Ζωή, therefore, properly denotes the *good of existence* as flowing directly from God, and carries us up to a higher conception of *life* than ψυχή, which seems to have a more legitimate reference to the *sensitive principle* in conjunction with which the true substratum of our being acts and manifests itself. It is in great measure by the ζωή that man is distinguished from the brute creation, which possesses the ψυχή, but not the ζωή. It is by this also that man is to be supposed preeminently to be conjoined to the Deity, and thus made secure of immortal existence, which is not to be conceived of brutes, because they lack the principle on which it is founded. Now it cannot, we think, be doubted that the phenomena of *sensation* are effected by means of the ψυχή even while connected with and pervading the bodily structure; for it is far from being clear, that the body, strictly speaking, is susceptible of any sensation whatever. A lifeless corpse is organically as perfect as a living body, yet it has no sensation. The sentient power has departed, but we know of nothing that requires the belief that in forsaking the body it loses any of its distinguishing attributes. But this point we shall consider more fully in the sequel.

The corresponding Latin terms for the vital and intellectual part of our nature, *animus—anima—spiritus*—are also obviously of the same etymological origin, *anima* being derived from *animus*, and this from ἄνεμος, *wind*, while *spiritus* comes directly from *spiro*, *to breathe, to blow*. The Latin, however, has still another word, *mens*, to which corresponds the English word *mind*, used in reference to the same subject. These terms signified originally that which *knows* or *understands*, and are derived from the root *mena*, *to know*, an etymon, which though lost in the European languages, is preserved like many of their common roots, in the Sanskrit, to which is to be traced the Greek μανθάνω, *he means*. The Greek νοῦς, also signifying *mind*, comes from the νοέω, *to know*.

Our common English word *soul* is of an origin somewhat difficult to be determined. Grimm (Grammatik, Theil II § 99) remarks that the German word for *soul*, at present *seele*, was anciently, in the Gothic of the third

USAGE OF נֶפֶשׁ, ψυχή, SOUL, ETC. 27

and fourth centuries, *saiv-a-la*, from which came in the eighth and ninth centuries *seul-a* and *sela*, whence *seele*, and in the Anglo-Saxon *sauv-el* (pron. *souv-el*), from which he thinks flows by easy sequence the English *soul*. The derivation of *saivala* from *saivan*, denoting the effect of a *violent wind* or *storm*, is highly probable, he observes, although in the ancient monuments we find the word *saivn* applied only to the *waving sea* The word *seele* might therefore have had originally a double import, as ἄνεμος, viz. that of *wind* and *spirit*. (*Schubert's Gesch. der Seele*, p. 716.)

Nothing is more remarkable than the fact that in all these languages the leading words designating the *soul* are from roots that have some relation to *air, wind, breath*. Still this relation is probably to be deemed of a *phenomenal* rather than of a *real* character, and founded upon the obvious sensible fact, that *breath* was the grand criterion of *life*. The *intrinsic nature* of the soul is not therefore at all disclosed by the import of the terms used to denote it. This we are left to discover, if possible, by such means as are within our reach. The object of our present inquiry however will be attained even if we should fall short of this.

In attempting a sytematic classification of the various senses of the word נֶפֶשׁ=ψυχή=*soul*, we shall commence with the somewhat peculiar usage that discloses itself in the first instances of its occurrence in the sacred text In the account of the creation in the first two chapters of Genesis we meet with the frequent use of נֶפֶשׁ, and always accompanied by חַיָּה *living*, although, according to Gesenius, this latter word is not an adjective, but a noun, and requiring the phrase to be literally rendered in English by *breath of life*. But we think the simple idea of *breath* scarcely comes up to the import of the word in this connexion. It rather denotes, we conceive, the inner, essential, constituent principle in which the life inheres that is indicated by the breath. But it is even in that sense evidently a concrete, and the established version *living creature* undoubtedly presents very fairly the leading import of the term, especially in reference to the animal tribes to which it is expressly applied. The Greek, however, invariably represents it by ψυχὴ ζῶσα, *living soul*, and this rendering our translators have adopted, Gen. 2. 7, where the creation of man is spoken of. Yet it is an important fact, which is necessarily lost sight of by the mere English reader, that precisely the same language is employed in reference to the creation of man and of beasts. They were both made ψυχία ζῶσαι, *living souls*. Whatever be the intrinsic nature of the *psychical* principle, both share it in common—a fact from which some have inferred that beasts are as immortal as man, and others that man is as mortal as beasts. But we shall see in the sequel that one inference is as erroneous as the other. While the ψυχὴ is not in itself immortal, and therefore secures not immortality to its brute possessors, it is made immortal in man by its connexion with the πνεῦμα, or *spirit*, an element which belongs to the human nature alone. But upon this part of the subject we shall treat more at length in another place. Our present object is to exhibit the usage of—

§ 2.

נֶפֶשׁ *in the sense of Living Creature, with the uniform accompaniment of* חַיָה.

Gen. 1. 20, "Let the waters bring forth abundantly *the moving creature that hath life* (שֶׁרֶץ נֶפֶשׁ חַיָה)."

This may be rendered by apposition, and collectively, *the living reptile, the living creature;* but Rosenmuller prefers the construction by regimen, *the swarming reptile of a living soul*, i. e possessed of a living soul; and this is countenanced by the Greek ἑρπετὰ ψυχῶν ζωσῶν, *creeping things of living souls* To the leading sense of the term it is not material which of the readings we adopt, and grammatical canons will warrant either. The idea of *life*, which is really native to the word, is heightened by the adjunct חָיָה.

Gen. 1. 21, "And God created great whales, and every *living creature* (נֶפֶשׁ חַיָּה) that moveth."

" 1. 24, "Let the earth bring forth the *living creature* (נֶפֶשׁ חַיָּה) after his kind."

" 1. 30, "To every thing that creepeth, wherein there is *life* (נֶפֶשׁ חַיָּה), I have given," &c.

" 2 7. "And the Lord God formed man of the dust of the ground, and breathed into his nostrils the *breath of life* (נִשְׁמַת חַיִּים *breath of lives*), and he *became a living soul* (לְנֶפֶשׁ חַיָּה—Gr. εἰς ψυχὴν ζῶσαν)."

Here we see that the more appropriate Heb. expression for simple *breath* is not נֶפֶשׁ, but נְשָׁמָה *neshâmâh*, which will be considered hereafter, though it is still unquestionable that נֶפֶשׁ is etymologically related to נָפַשׁ to *breathe* or *blow*. But only a single instance occurs in the biblical text where it is rendered *breath*, and there it is spoken of God; Job, 41. 13, "His *breath* (נַפְשׁוֹ) kindleth coals." In another passage of Job, ch 11. 20, it is rendered by *ghost*, though the margin has *breath*—"The hope of the wicked shall be as the *giving up of the ghost* (מַפַּח נֶפֶשׁ, *the breathing forth of the life* or *soul*. Marg. *a puff of breath*)." So also Jer. 15. 9, "She that hath borne seven languisheth, she hath given up the *ghost* (נֶפֶשׁ)." These passages come the nearest of any that can be specified to the sense of simple *breath*, and yet they all of them, except Job 11. 13, evidently carry the mind to the deeper idea of *life* or *soul*.

Gen. 2 19, "And whatsoever Adam called any *living creature* (נֶפֶשׁ חַיָּה), that was the name thereof."

" 9. 12, "This is the token of the covenant which I make between me and you, and every *living creature* (נֶפֶשׁ חַיָּה)."

" 9. 16, "That I may remember the everlasting covenant between God and every *living creature* (נֶפֶשׁ חַיָּה)."

§ 3

נֶפֶשׁ *in the sense of Life,* ψυχή, *Anima, the Vital Principle, by which the Body lives.*

The usage under this head prevails very extensively in the sacred writers, and in our version the rendering is interchangeably *life* and *soul,* the latter however being the English equivalent more generally adopted. The Greek has almost invariably ψυχή. How much more is legitimately implied in the term than the simple idea of *vitality,* exclusive of *thought* and *feeling,* may no doubt be a matter on which difference of opinion may be entertained. Our object, however, is to present the usage, as a matter of fact, with all the discrimination attainable, while at the same time we are fully aware that many of the passages which we may cite under this head another would refer to another. We can perhaps only hope to approximate to a just classification.

Gen. 9. 4, "But the flesh *with the life thereof* (בְּנַפְשׁוֹ), which is the blood thereof, shall ye not eat."

We are not probably to understand this as intended to affirm it as a physiological fact, that the *life* is pre-eminently seated in the *blood,* which was formerly held by some physiologists, but is now discarded, but simply as intimating the close connexion between the possession of the due quantity of blood and the possession of life, inasmuch as if the blood be shed the life is gone.

Gen. 9. 5, "And surely your blood of *your lives* (לְנַפְשֹׁתֵיכֶם) will I require: at the hand of every beast will I require it, and at the hand of man, at the hand of every man's brother will I require the *life* (נֶפֶשׁ) of man."

" 19 17, "Escape for *thy life* (נַפְשֶׁךָ)."

" " 19, "Thou hast magnified thy mercy, ... in saving *my life* (נַפְשִׁי)."

" 32. 30, "I have seen God face to face, and *my life* (נַפְשִׁי) is preserved."

Gen. 35 18, "And it came to pass as her *soul* (נַפְשָׁהּ) was in departing."

This might doubtless as properly have been rendered *life*, which is said to *depart* at death, though it is nowhere said to expire or become extinct.

" 37 21, "Let us not kill *him* (נֶפֶשׁ—Lit *let us not smite or kill him, soul*, i e. as to his soul or life)."

" 44 30, "Seeing that *his life* (נַפְשׁוֹ) is bound up in the child's *life* (נֶפֶשׁ)."

Ex. 4 19, "All the men are dead which sought *thy life* (נַפְשֶׁךָ)."

" 21 23, "And if any mischief follow, then thou shalt give *life for life* (נֶפֶשׁ תַּחַת נֶפֶשׁ)."

" " 30, "For the ransom of *his life* (נַפְשׁוֹ)."

Lev. 17 11, "For the *life* (נֶפֶשׁ) of the flesh is in the blood." Comp v 14

" 24. 17, "He that killeth *any man* (נֶפֶשׁ אָדָם—Lit. *that smiteth the life of a man*)."

" 24 18, "He that killeth a beast shall make it good *beast for beast* (נֶפֶשׁ תַּחַת נֶפֶשׁ *life for life*)."

The established rendering undoubtedly gives the true sense, but it would have been better to have translated according to the letter, as we feel at once the violence of rendering נֶפֶשׁ by *beast*.

Num 35 31, "Ye shall take no satisfaction for the *life* (נֶפֶשׁ) of a murderer."

Deut 12 23, "The blood is the *life* (נֶפֶשׁ); and thou mayest not eat the *life* (נֶפֶשׁ)."

" 19 6, "Lest the avenger of blood . . . . slay *him* (נֶפֶשׁ —Lit. *smite him as to the life*)"

" " *Life* shall go for *life* (נֶפֶשׁ—נֶפֶשׁ)."

" 22 26, "As when a man riseth against his neighbor, and slayeth *him* (נֶפֶשׁ—Lit. *smiteth him as to the life*)."

" 24. 6, "For he taketh a man's *life* (נֶפֶשׁ) to pledge."

Josh 2. 13, "Deliver *our souls* (נַפְשֹׁתֵינוּ) from death," i. e. our *lives*.

Josh. 2. 14, "*Our lives* (נפשנו) for yours"
" 9. 21, "We were sore afraid *of our lives* (לנפשתינו, *for our lives*)."
Judg. 5. 18, "A people that jeoparded *their lives* (נפשו) unto death."
" 12. 3, "I put *my life* (נפשי) in my hand."
Ruth, 4. 15, 'A restorer of thy *life* (נפש)"
1 Sam. 19. 5, "For he did put *his life* (נפשו) in his hand."
" " 11, "If thou save not *thy life* (נפשך) to-night."
" 22. 23, "He that seeketh *my life* (נפשי) seeketh *thy life* (נפשך)"
" 23. 15, "Saul was come out to seek *his life* (נפשו)."
" 24. 11, "Thou huntest *my soul* (נפשי) to take it," i. e. *my life*.
" 26. 21, " Because *my soul* (נפשי) was precious in thine eyes this day," i. e. *my life*
" 26. 24, " And behold, as *thy life* (נפשך) was much set by this day in mine eyes, so let *my life* (נפשי) be much set by in the eyes of the Lord"
" 28. 9, "Wherefore then layest thou a snare for *my life* (נפשי)?"
2 Sam. 1. 9, "*My life* (נפשי) is yet whole in me."
" 4. 8, "Behold the head of Ish-bo-sheth . . . which sought *thy life* (נפשך)"
" 14. 7, "That we may kill him *for the life* (בנפש) of his brother whom he slew."
" 16. 11, "Seeketh *my life* (נפשי)"
" 18. 13, "I should have wrought falsehood against *my own life* (בנפשי)"
" 19. 5, "Which this day have saved *thy life* (נפשך), the *lives* (נפש) of thy sons . . . and the *lives* (נפש) of thy wives, and the *lives* (נפש) of thy concubines."
" 23. 17, "The blood of the men which went *in jeopardy of their lives* (בנפשותם *with their lives*)" So also 1 Chron. 11. 19.

USAGE OF נֶפֶשׁ, ψυχη, SOUL, ETC.   33

1 Kings, 1. 12, "That thou mayest save *thine own life* (נַפְשֶׁךָ), and the *life* (נֶפֶשׁ) of thy son Solomon."
" 2. 23, "If Adonijah have not spoken this word against *his own life* (בְּנַפְשׁוֹ)."
" 3. 11, "Nor hast asked the *life* (נֶפֶשׁ) of thine enemies."
" 19. 2, "If I make not *thy life* (נַפְשְׁךָ) as the *life* (נֶפֶשׁ) of one of them."
" 19. 3, "He arose and went for *his life* (נַפְשׁוֹ)."
" 19. 4, "And requested for *himself* (נַפְשׁוֹ, for *his life*) that he might die; and said, It is enough; now, O Lord, take away *my life* (נַפְשִׁי)."
" 20. 31, "Peradventure he will save *thy life* (נַפְשֶׁךָ)"
" 20. 39, "Then shall *thy life* (נַפְשְׁךָ) be for *his life* (נַפְשׁוֹ)" So also v. 42. 2 Kings, 10. 24.
2 Kings, 1. 13, "Let *my life* (נַפְשִׁי) and the *life* (נֶפֶשׁ) of these fifty thy servants be precious in thy sight." So also v. 14.
" 7. 7, "And fled for *their life* (בְּנַפְשָׁם)."
Est. 7. 3, "Let *my life* (נַפְשִׁי) be given me at my petition."
" 7. 7, "Haman stood up to make request for *his life* (נַפְשׁוֹ)"
" 8. 11, "To stand for *their lives* (נַפְשָׁם)." So also chap. 9. 16.
Job, 2. 4, "All that a man hath will he give for *his life* (נַפְשׁוֹ)."
" 2. 6, "Behold, he is in thine hand, but save *his life* (נַפְשׁוֹ)."
" 12. 10, "In whose hand is the *soul* (נֶפֶשׁ, *life*) of every living thing, and the breath of all mankind."
" 31. 39, "Have caused the owners thereof to lose their *life* (נֶפֶשׁ)." See a parallel to this, Prov. 1. 19.
Ps. 35. 4, "Let them be confounded and put to shame that seek after *my soul* (נַפְשִׁי)."

3

This passage may stand as the representative of a large number occurring in the Psalms, where the same expression in the original is sometimes rendered by "seeking the *soul*," and sometimes by "seeking the *life*." The import is undoubtedly to seek the *life* with a view to destroy it. We would therefore render the phrase uniformly by *life* instead of *soul*. In like manner the phrase "laying wait for the *soul*," we take to be equivalent to "laying wait for the *life*" with a persecuting or murderous intent. So again, *preserving, delivering, redeeming the soul*, is, we suppose, to be understood of performing these offices for the *life*, though it is possible there may be cases of this kind where a higher meaning may be attached to the word *soul*, and one that shall bring it under a subsequent head.

Prov. 1. 18, "They lurk privily *for their own lives* (לְנַפְשֹׁתָם)."
" 6. 26, "The adulteress will hunt for the precious *life* (נֶפֶשׁ)."
" 7. 23, "And knoweth not that it is *for his life* (בְּנַפְשׁוֹ)."
" 12. 10, "A righteous man regardeth the *life* (נֶפֶשׁ) of his beast."
" 13. 3, "He that keepeth his mouth keepeth *his life* (נַפְשׁוֹ)."
" 13. 8, "The ransom of a man's *life* (נֶפֶשׁ) are his riches."

Is 15. 4, "*His life* (נַפְשׁוֹ) shall be grievous unto him."
Jer. 21. 9, "*His life* (נַפְשׁוֹ) shall be unto him for a prey." So also ch. 38. 18—45.
" 48. 6, "Flee, save *your lives* (נַפְשְׁכֶם)."

Lam. 2. 12, "When their *soul* (נֶפֶשׁ) was poured out into their mother's bosom," i. e. their *life*. This is understood by some to be equivalent to the *blood*.
" 2. 19, "Lift up thine hands toward him for the *life* (נֶפֶשׁ) of thy young children."
" 5. 9, "We gat our bread with the peril of *our lives* (נַפְשֵׁנוּ)."

Ezek 32. 10, "They shall tremble at every moment, every man *for his own life* (לְנַפְשׁוֹ)."

" 47. 9, "And it shall come to pass that *every thing that liveth* (כֹּל נֶפֶשׁ חַיָּה, *every soul of life*) shall live."

Jon 1. 14, "Let us not perish for this man's *life* (נֶפֶשׁ)."

" 4. 3, "Take, I beseech thee, *my life* (נַפְשִׁי)."

Mat 2. 20, "For they are dead which sought the young child's *life* (ψυχήν)."

" 10. 39, "He that findeth his *life* (ψυχήν) shall lose it; and he that loseth his *life* (ψυχήν) for my sake, shall find it." So also ch. 16. 25

Mr. Barnes remarks upon this passage that "the word *life* is used in two senses. The meaning may be expressed thus He that is anxious to secure his *temporal* life, or his comfort and security here, shall lose *eternal* life; or shall fail of heaven. He that is willing to lose his comfort and *life* here, for my sake, shall find everlasting life, or shall be saved." In either case there is a superadded sense of *enjoyment*, which is frequently to be recognized in the use of the word *life*, both in the Old Testament and the New.

Mat. 16 26, "For what is a man profited if he shall gain the whole world and lose his own *soul* (ψυχήν, *life*), or what shall a man give in exchange for his *soul* (ψυχήν, *life*)?"

In the parallel passage, Luke 9. 25, it is said, "For what is a man advantaged, if he gain the whole world, *and lose himself*, or be cast away?" The word *life* or *soul*, therefore, in this connection must doubtless be taken in the same sense with נֶפֶשׁ No 6, implying that which constitutes the *ipseity* or *essential self* of a man. This is the highest import of the word *soul*, and involves more than the simple idea of *physical life*. There is, therefore, some ground for rendering ψυχή by *soul* here, though the same term is rendered in the preceding verse by *life*.

Mat. 20. 28, "Even as the Son of man came not to be ministered unto, but to minister, and to give his *life* (ψυχήν) a ransom for many." So Mark, 8. 45.

Mark, 3. 4, "Is it lawful to do good on the Sabbath-days, or to do evil? to save *life* (ψυχὴν), or to kill?"

Luke, 14. 26, "If any man come to me, and hate not his father, and mother, and wife, and brethren, and sisters, yea, and his own *life* (ψυχὴν) also, he cannot be my disciple."

John, 10. 11, "I am the good shepherd that giveth his *life* (ψυχὴν) for the sheep." So also ch. 10, 15.

" 13. 37, " I will lay down my *life* (ψυχὴν) for thy sake." So v. 38, and 15. 13.

Acts, 15. 26, "Men that have hazarded their *lives* (ψυχὰς) for the name of our Lord Jesus Christ."

" 20. 10, "Trouble not yourselves, for his *life* (ψυχὴ) is in him."

" 20. 24, "Neither count I my *life* (ψυχὴν) dear unto myself."

" 27. 10, "I perceive that this voyage will be with hurt and much damage, not only of the lading and ship, but also of our *lives* (ψυχῶν)."

" 27. 22, "There shall be no loss of any man's *life* (ψυχῆς) among you, but only of the ship."

Rom. 11. 3, " I am left alone, and they seek my *life* (ψυχὴν)"

" 16. 4, "Who have for my *life* (ψυχῆς) laid down their own necks." So 1 John, 3. 16.

Phil. 2. 30, "For the work of Christ he was nigh unto death, not regarding his *life* (ψυχῇ)."

Rev. 8. 9, "And the third part of the creatures which were in the sea and had *life* (ψυχὰς, *souls*), died."

" 12. 11, "And they loved not their *lives* (ψυχὰς) unto the death." This, however, may be rendered *souls* in the sense of *themselves*.

The above list of citations contains nearly all the prominent instances to be found in the Old and New Testaments of the use of the word נפש, ψυχὴ, in the sense of *life*. The passages omitted are mostly repetitions of certain texts that occur in our catalogue. The Greek rendering of נפש,

we believe is, in every case, ψυχή. The English representative *soul* occurs in a few instances, but the dominant term is correctly *life*. The most obvious idea which is to be attached to *life* in these connexions is simply that of the *animal or vital principle* by which a living is distinguished from a dead body. As the term is applied equally to men and to beasts, there is no necessary implication, as far as these passages are concerned, of those *intellectual and moral attributes* usually indicated by the word *soul*, and which constitute that element of our being of which *immortality* is more properly predicated. We shall find, indeed, in the classifications that follow, that the word is used extensively in a higher sense and one that involves the import of *animus* as well as *anima*, or of the *rational faculties* peculiar to man as standing at the head of the terrestrial order of creatures In pursuing, however, the train of development which we have marked out, we encounter a peculiar difficulty in discriminating accurately between the purely *intellectual* and the *emotional* or *sensitive* part of our nature, alluded to in a great variety of texts. That the term in its genuine significance points often to that principle which is the seat of *sensation* and *affection*, rather than of *intellection*, we think is undoubted. Still as these principles co-exist and co-act together by the very constitution of our being, it is not perhaps to be expected that the line which separates their respective spheres should be made, by the sacred writers, very distinctly conspicuous. We can hardly expect, therefore, that the following, or in fact that any, classification can carry with it such ample evidence of its truth as to preclude all doubt. The usage of terms in all languages frequently varies by such nice and imperceptible shades, and, according to the genius of the writer or the scope of the context, their different senses so glide into and blend with each other, that the attempt to discriminate them is like the attempt to mark the precise line of separation between the tints of the rainbow. All that we can aim at is the nearest possible approximation to a correct estimate of the force of the term in question in its different textual relations.

§ 4.

נֶפֶשׁ *as the Seat of Sensation, the Subject of Bodily Appetites, Desires, and the various kinds of Sensual or Animal Affections.*

Ex. 15. 9, "*My lust* (נַפְשִׁי, *my soul,*) shall be satisfied upon them"

Num. 21. 5, *Our soul* (נַפְשֵׁנוּ) loatheth this light bread."

Deut. 12. 15, 20, 21, "Whatsoever *thy soul* (נַפְשְׁךָ) lusteth after."

"   12 20, "*Thy soul* (נַפְשְׁךָ) longeth to eat flesh"

"   14. 16, "Whatsoever *thy soul* (נַפְשְׁךָ) lusteth after, .. whatsoever *thy soul* (נַפְשֶׁךָ) desireth"

"   13. 6, "With all the desire of *his mind* (נַפְשׁוֹ)."

"   21. 14, "If thou have no delight in her, thou shalt let her go *whither she will* (לְנַפְשָׁהּ, lit. *to her soul).*"

   24 15, "For he is poor, and setteth *his heart* (נַפְשׁוֹ, *his soul*) upon it."

1 Sam. 2. 16, "Take as much as *thy soul* (נַפְשְׁךָ) desireth."

Job, 6. 7, "The things that *my soul* (נַפְשִׁי) refused to touch are as my sorrowful meat."

"   24. 12, "And the *soul* (נֶפֶשׁ) of the wounded crieth out." That which is the seat of sensation.

"   33 20, "So that his life abhorreth bread, and *his soul* (נַפְשׁוֹ) dainty meat"

Ps 10. 3, "The wicked boasteth of *his heart's* (נַפְשׁוֹ) desire."

"   35. 13, "I humbled *my soul* (נַפְשִׁי) with fasting."

"   69. 1, "Save me, O God; for the waters are come in unto *my soul* (נַפְשִׁי)." My troubles reach the inmost seat of sensation.

Psalm 78. 18, "They tempted God in their hearts by asking meat *for their lust* (לְנַפְשָׁם, *for their souls*)."
" 105. 18. " Whose feet they hurt with fetters ; *he was laid in iron* (בַּרְזֶל בָּאָה נַפְשׁוֹ, *his soul came into iron*) "
" 107. 9, " For he satisfieth the longing *soul* (נֶפֶשׁ), and filleth the hungry *soul* (נֶפֶשׁ) with goodness." With bodily blessings.
" 107 18, " *Their soul* נַפְשָׁם) abhorreth all manner of meat."
Prov. 6. 30, "Men do not despise a thief if he steal to satisfy *his soul* (נַפְשׁוֹ i. e. *his appetite*) when he is
" hungry."
" 10. 3, " Thou wilt not suffer the *soul* (נֶפֶשׁ) of the righteous to famish."

That this refers to a supply of the *temporal* wants of the righteous, is obvious from the remaining clause of the verse, " but he casteth away the substance of the wicked "
Prov 13. 4, " The *soul* (נֶפֶשׁ) of the sluggard desireth and hath nothing; but the *soul* (נֶפֶשׁ) of the diligent shall be made fat."
" 13. 25, " The righteous eateth to the satisfying of his *soul* (נַפְשׁוֹ)."
" 16. 17, "Pleasant words are as an honey-comb, sweet to the *soul* (נֶפֶשׁ), and health to the bones."
" 19. 15, " An idle *soul* (נֶפֶשׁ) shall suffer hunger."
" 22. 23, "For the Lord will plead their cause, and spoil the *soul* (נֶפֶשׁ) of those that spoiled them."
" 23. 2, " Put a knife to thy throat if thou be a man given to *appetite* (נֶפֶשׁ, to *soul*)."
" 25. 13, " For he refresheth the *soul* (נֶפֶשׁ) of his masters."
" 25. 25, " As cold waters to a thirsty *soul* (נֶפֶשׁ), so is good news from a far country."
" 27. 7, " The full *soul* (נֶפֶשׁ) loatheth an honey-comb; but to the hungry *soul* (נֶפֶשׁ) every bitter thing is sweet."

Eccl. 2. 24, "That he should make his *soul* (נַפְשׁוֹ) enjoy good in his labor." Marg. "Or, delight his senses."
" 6. 2, "A man to whom God hath given riches, wealth, and honor, so that he wanteth nothing for his *soul* (נַפְשׁוֹ) "
" 6. 3, " And his *soul* (נַפְשׁוֹ) be not filled with good."
" 6. 7, " All the labor of man is for his mouth, and yet the *appetite* (נֶפֶשׁ, *soul*) is not filled."
Is. 29. 8, "As when an hungry man dreameth, and behold he eateth; but he awaketh, and his *soul* (נַפְשׁוֹ) is empty: or as when a thirsty man dreameth, and behold he drinketh ; but he awaketh, and behold he is faint, and his *soul* (נַפְשׁוֹ) hath appetite."
" 32. 6, "To make empty the *soul* (נֶפֶשׁ) of the hungry."
" 56. 11, " They are *greedy dogs* (עַזֵּי נֶפֶשׁ, dogs *strong of soul*, i. e. of ravenous appetite)."
" 58. 11, "The Lord shall satisfy thy *soul* (נַפְשׁוֹ) in drought."
Jer. 31. 12, " *Their soul* (נַפְשָׁם) shall be as a watered garden."

That the idea here is not primarily that of *spiritual* abundance, will be obvious upon inspection of the whole verse. So also in the two texts that immediately follow.

Jer. 31. 14, "I will satiate the *soul* (נֶפֶשׁ) of the priests with fatness"
" 31. 25, "I have satiated the weary *soul* (נֶפֶשׁ), and I have replenished every sorrowful *soul* (נֶפֶשׁ)."
" 50. 19, "And I will bring Israel again to his habitation, and he shall feed on Carmel and Bashan, and his *soul* (נַפְשׁוֹ) shall be satisfied upon Mount Ephraim and Gilead."
Mic. 7. 1, " *My soul* (נַפְשִׁי) desired the first ripe fruit."
Mat. 6. 25, " Take no thought for your *life* ($\psi v \chi \eta v$), what ye shall eat," &c.—" Is not the *life* ($\psi v \chi \eta$) more than meat, and the body than raiment ?"

Luke, 2 3, "Yea, a sword shall pierce through thine own *soul* (ψυχήν) also"

We are not entirely confident that this passage ranges itself most naturally under this head. We give it here from its parallelism with Ps. 105 18, "He was laid in iron (Heb. his *soul* came into iron)."

Luke, 12. 19, 20, "I will say to my *soul* (ψυχή), Soul (ψυχή), thou hast much goods laid up for many years; take thine ease, eat, drink, and be merry. But God said unto him, Thou fool, this night shall thy *soul* (ψυχή) be required of thee."

" 12 22, 23, "Take no thought for your *life* (ψυχήν), what ye shall eat; neither for your body, what ye shall put on. The *life* (ψυχή) is more than meat, and the body than raiment."

The foregoing list of quotations might perhaps be increased by the addition of a few more which as properly pertain to this department as most of those actually given; and it might perhaps be diminished by the subtraction of several that would as properly come under another head. But we believe it contains, on the whole, a pretty fair exhibit of the usage which recognizes the word *soul*, as expressing the seat of what may be termed—whether correctly or not—*corporeal sensation and affection*, and with which the idea of *intellectual attributes* is not necessarily connected. Under the next division we are advanced to a higher sense.

§ 5.

נֶפֶשׁ *in the sense of Animus, Rational Soul, Mind, and considered as the Seat of various Passions, Emotions, and Affections pertaining to a Rational Being, such as Love, Joy, Fear, Sorrow, Hope, Hatred, Revenge, Contempt*, &c.

Gen. 23. 8, "*If it be your mind* (אִם־יֵשׁ אֶת נַפְשְׁכֶם, *if it be with your mind or soul*) *that I should bury my dead.*"

Gen. 34. 3, "*His soul* (נַפְשׁוֹ) clave unto Dinah." So also v. 8.

" 42. 21, " We saw the anguish of *his soul* (נַפְשׁוֹ)."

Ex. 23 9, Ye know the *heart* (נֶפֶשׁ, the soul, i. e. *the feelings*) of a stranger."

Lev. 10 29, " Ye shall afflict *your souls* (נַפְשֹׁתֵיכֶם)." So also ch. 23. 27. 29. 32, and often elsewhere.

" 26. 15, " If *your soul* (נַפְשְׁכֶם) abhor my judgments."

" 26. 16, " And cause sorrow of *heart* (נֶפֶשׁ)."

" 26. 43, " *Their soul* (נַפְשָׁם) abhorred my statutes."

Num. 21. 4, " The *soul* (נֶפֶשׁ) of the people was much discouraged."

Deut. 4. 9, " Keep *thy soul* (נַפְשְׁךָ) diligently."

" 4. 29, " Seek him with all *thy soul* (נַפְשְׁךָ)."

" 6. 5, " With all *thy soul* (נַפְשְׁךָ) and all thy might." So also ch. 10. 12, and often elsewhere.

" 11. 18, " In your heart and in *your soul* (נַפְשְׁכֶם)."

" 13. 16, " With all the desire of his *mind* (נֶפֶשׁ)."

" 28. 65. " The Lord shall give . . . . thee sorrow of *mind* (נֶפֶשׁ)."

Judg. 16. 16, " *His soul* (נַפְשׁוֹ) was vexed unto death."

1 Sam. 1. 10, " She was in bitterness of *soul* (נֶפֶשׁ)."

" 2. 33, " To grieve *thine heart* (נַפְשְׁךָ)."

" 18. 3, " He loved him as *his own soul* (נַפְשׁוֹ)."

" 22. 2, " Every one that was *discontented* (מַר נֶפֶשׁ, *bitter of soul*)."

" 30. 6, " The *soul* (נֶפֶשׁ) of all the people was grieved."

2 Sam. 5. 8, " That are hated of David's *soul* (נֶפֶשׁ)."

" 17. 8, " They be chafed in their *minds* (מָרֵי נֶפֶשׁ, *bitter of soul*)."

2 Kings, 9. 15, " If it be *your minds* (נַפְשְׁכֶם), then let none go."

1 Chron. 28. 9, " Serve him with a perfect heart and a willing *mind* (נֶפֶשׁ)"

Job, 3. 20, "Wherefore is light given to him that is in misery, and life unto the bitter in *soul* (נֶפֶשׁ)?"

" 7. 11, "I will complain in the bitterness of *my soul* (נַפְשִׁי)." So also ch. 10. 1.

" 7. 15, "*My soul* (נַפְשִׁי) chooseth strangling."

" 10. 1, "*My soul* (נַפְשִׁי) is weary of life."

" 14. 22, "And *his soul* (נַפְשׁוֹ) within him shall mourn."

" 19. 2, "How long will ye vex *my soul* (נַפְשִׁי)?"

" 30. 25, "Was not *my soul* (נַפְשִׁי) grieved for the poor?"

Ps. 6. 3, "*My soul* (נַפְשִׁי) is also sore vexed."

" 10. 3, "The wicked boasteth of *his soul's* (נַפְשׁוֹ) desire."

" 11. 5, "Him that loveth violence *his soul* (נַפְשׁוֹ) hateth."

" 27. 12, "Deliver me not over unto the *will* (נַפְשׁוֹ) of mine enemies." See also ch. 41. 2.

" 33. 20, "*Our soul* (נַפְשֵׁנוּ) waiteth for the Lord."

" 35. 9, "And *my soul* (נַפְשִׁי) shall be joyful in the Lord."

" 42. 1, "So panteth *my soul* (נַפְשִׁי) after thee."

" 42. 6, "*My soul* (נַפְשִׁי) is cast down within me." So v. 5; ch. 43. 5, 44. 25; 57. 6.

" 57. 1, "*My soul* (נַפְשִׁי) trusteth in thee."

" 63. 8, "*My soul* (נַפְשִׁי) followeth hard after thee."

" 77. 2, "*My soul* (נַפְשִׁי) refuseth to be comforted."

" 84. 2, "*My soul* (נַפְשִׁי) longeth . . . . for the courts of the Lord."

" 86. 4, "Rejoice the *soul* (נֶפֶשׁ) of thy servant."

" 88. 3, "*My soul* (נַפְשִׁי) is full of troubles."

" 94. 19, "Thy comforts delight *my soul* (נַפְשִׁי)."

" 107. 26, "*Their soul* (נַפְשָׁם) is melted because of trouble."

" 119. 20, "*My soul* (נַפְשִׁי) breaketh for the longing it hath unto thy judgments."

" 119. 25, "*My soul* (נַפְשִׁי) cleaveth unto the dust."

SCRIPTURAL PSYCHOLOGY.

Ps. 119. 28, "*My soul* (נַפְשִׁי) melteth for heaviness.'
" 123 4, "*Our soul* (נַפְשֵׁנוּ) is exceedingly filled with the scorning of those that are at ease "
" 43. 12, "Destroy all them that afflict *my soul* (נַפְשִׁי)."
Prov 2. 10, "Knowledge is pleasant to the *soul* (נֶפֶשׁ)."
" 113. 19, "The desire accomplished is sweet to the *soul* (נֶפֶשׁ)."
" 21. 10, "The *soul* (נֶפֶשׁ) of the wicked desireth evil."
" 28. 25, "He that is of a proud *heart* (נֶפֶשׁ)."
" 29. 17, "He shall give delight unto *thy soul* (נַפְשֶׁךָ) "
" 31. 6, "Give wine to those that be of *heavy hearts* (מָרֵי נָפֶשׁ, *bitter of soul*)."
Eccl. 6. 3, "And his *soul* (נַפְשׁוֹ) be not filled with good "
Cant. 3. 1, "O thou, whom *my soul* (נַפְשִׁי) loveth." So also 2, 3, 4.
Is. 61. 10, "*My soul* (נַפְשִׁי) shall be joyful in God."
Jer. 4 31, "*My soul* (נַפְשִׁי) is wearied because of murderers."
" 6. 16, "Ye shall find rest for *your souls* (נַפְשְׁכֶם)."
Lam. 1. 16, "The comforter that should relieve *my soul* (נַפְשִׁי)."
" 3 51, "Mine eye affecteth *my heart* (נַפְשִׁי)."
Ezek. 23. 17, "*Her mind* (נַפְשָׁהּ) was alienated from them " So also vs. 18, 22, 28.
" 24. 21. "That which *your soul* (נַפְשְׁכֶם) pitieth "
" 25. 6, "Rejoiced in *heart* (נֶפֶשׁ) with all thy despite."
" 25. 15, "Taken vengeance with a despiteful *heart* (נֶפֶשׁ)."
" 36. 5, "Which have appointed my land . . . with despiteful *minds* (נֶפֶשׁ)."
Hos. 4. 8, "They set *their heart* (נַפְשָׁם) on their iniquity."
Jon. 2. 7, "When *my soul* (נַפְשִׁי) fainted."
Mich. 7. 3, "He uttereth his *mischievous desire* (הַוַּת נַפְשׁוֹ, *the mischief of his soul*)."
Hab. 2. 4, "Behold *his soul* (נַפְשׁוֹ) which is lifted up, is not upright in him "

Hab. 1. 5, " Who enlargeth his *desire* (הִרְחִיב) as hell."

Mat. 11. 29, " Ye shall find rest for your *souls* ($\psi v \chi \alpha \iota \varsigma$)."

" 22. 37, " Thou shalt love the Lord thy God with all thy heart, and with all thy *soul* ($\psi v \chi \eta$), and with all thy mind." So Luke, 10. 27.

" 26 38, " My *soul* ($\psi v \chi \eta$) is exceeding sorrowful, even unto death."

John, 10 24, " How long dost thou make us to doubt ($\tilde{\epsilon}\omega\varsigma$ $\pi\acute{o}\tau\epsilon$ $\tau\grave{\eta}\nu$ $\psi v\chi\grave{\eta}\nu$ $\eta\mu\omega\nu$ $\alpha\iota\varrho\epsilon\iota\varsigma$, *how long dost thou hold our soul* in suspense) ?"

" 12. 27, " Now is my *soul* ($\psi v \chi \eta$) troubled."

Acts, 14. 2, " But the unbelieving Jews stirred up the Gentiles, and made their *minds* ($\psi v \chi \alpha \varsigma$, *souls*) evil affected against the brethren."

" 14 22, " Confirming the *souls* ($\psi v \chi \alpha \varsigma$) of the disciples."

" 15 24, " Forasmuch as we have heard, that certain which went out from us, have troubled you with words, subverting your *souls* ($\psi v \chi \alpha \varsigma$)."

2 Cor. 1. 23, " Moreover, I call God for a record upon my *soul* ($\psi v \chi \grave{\eta} \nu$) "

Eph. 6. 6, " As the servants of Christ, doing the will of God from the *heart* ($\psi v \chi \hat{\eta} \varsigma$, *soul*)."

Phil. 1. 27, " That ye stand fast in one spirit, with one *mind* ($\psi v \chi \hat{\eta}$) striving together for the faith of the gospel."

Col 3 23, " Whatsoever ye do, do it *heartily* ($\dot{\epsilon}\kappa$ $\tau\hat{\eta}\varsigma$ $\psi v\chi\hat{\eta}\varsigma$, *from the soul*), as to the Lord."

1 Thes. 5 23, " I pray God your whole spirit, *soul* ($\psi v \chi \grave{\eta}$), and body, be preserved blameless."

Heb. 4. 12, " Piercing even to the dividing asunder of *soul* ($\psi v \chi \hat{\eta} \varsigma$) and spirit."

" 6. 19, " Which hope we have as an anchor of the *soul* ($\psi v \chi \hat{\eta} \varsigma$)."

" 10. 39, " Of them that believe to the saving of the *soul* ($\psi v \chi \hat{\eta} \varsigma$)." So also 1 Pet. 1. 9.

Heb. 12. 3, "Lest ye be weary and faint in your *minds* (ψυχαῖς)."
" 13. 17, "For they watch for your *souls* (ψυχῶν) as they that must give account."
1 Pet. 1. 22, "Seeing ye have purified your *souls* (ψυχὰς) in obeying the truth."
" 2. 11, "Abstain from fleshly lusts which war against the *soul* (ψυχῆς)."
" 2. 25, "But are now returned unto the Shepherd and Bishop of your *souls* (ψυχῶν)."
" 4. 19, "Let them commit the keeping of their *souls* (ψυχῶν) to him in well doing."
2 Pet. 2. 8, "Vexed his righteous *soul* (ψυχὴν) from day to day."

§ 6.

נפש *in the sense of Person.*

The passages are very numerous in which the word נפש is employed as a concrete for the *man* as mainly distinguished by the possession of a *soul*, which is to be regarded as the true constituent of his *personality*, whatever may be its *essential nature*, of which no intimation is given in the term itself. A perfectly equivalent usage obtains in our language, as nothing is more common than to speak of a multitude of *persons* as a multitude of *souls*. Thus Shakspeare, speaking of a vessel that was shipwrecked, says she went down, and "all the freighting *souls* within her." Thus too we speak of the population of a city or country as amounting to so many *souls*.

Gen. 12. 5, "And all the *souls* (col. sing. נפש *soul*) that they had gotten in Haran," i. e. *persons*.
" 14. 21, "Give me the *persons* (נפש) and take the goods to thyself."
" 17. 44, "That *soul* (נפש) shall be cut off from his people."

USAGE OF נֶפֶשׁ, ψυχή, SOUL, ETC.

Gen. 36. 6, "And Esau took . . . all the *persons* (נַפְשׁוֹת, Gr. σώματα, *bodies*) of his house."

It doubtless appears singular that the term which in the Hebrew stands for *soul* should have been rendered in Greek by the usual word for *bodies*. But as *soul* and *body* are the two grand constituents of man, so he may be, as he is, sometimes denominated from the one, and sometimes from the other.

Gen. 46. 18, "These she bare . . sixteen *souls* (נֶפֶשׁ)." So also vs. 22, 25, 26, 27.

Ex. 1. 5, "All the *souls* (נֶפֶשׁ) that came out of the loins of Jacob were seventy *souls* (נֶפֶשׁ)."

" 12. 14, "According to the number of the *souls* (נְפָשׁוֹת)."

" 12. 15, "That *soul* (נֶפֶשׁ) shall be cut off from Israel." So v. 19, ch. 31. 14, and often elsewhere.

" 16. 16, ("According to) the number of *your persons* (נַפְשֹׁתֵיכֶם)."

Lev. 2. 1. "And when any (נֶפֶשׁ, *a soul*) will offer a male offering."

" 4. 2, "If a *soul* (נֶפֶשׁ) shall sin through ignorance."

" 4. 17, "If *any one* (נֶפֶשׁ marg. *any soul*) of the common people sin."

" 5. 2, "If a *soul* (נֶפֶשׁ) touch any unclean thing." So v. 4, "If a *soul* (נֶפֶשׁ) swear" v. 15, "If a *soul* (נֶפֶשׁ) commit a trespass." So in a multitude of other instances.

" 17. 12, "No *soul* (נֶפֶשׁ) of you shall eat blood."

" 17. 15, "Every *soul* (נֶפֶשׁ) that eateth that which died."

" 20. 6, "I will even set my face against that *soul* (נֶפֶשׁ)."

" 21. 11, "If the priest buy any *soul* (נֶפֶשׁ)."

" 23. 30, "Whatsoever *soul* (נֶפֶשׁ) it be that doeth any work in that same day, the same *soul* (נֶפֶשׁ) will I destroy."

" 29. 2, "The *persons* (נֶפֶשׁ) shall be for the Lord."

Num. 5. 6, "And that *person* (נֶפֶשׁ) be guilty."
" 15. 30, "But the *soul* (נֶפֶשׁ) that doeth aught presumptuously."
" 19. 18, "Shall sprinkle it upon the *persons* (נֶפֶשׁ) that were there."
" 31. 19, "Whosoever hath killed *any person* (נֶפֶשׁ)"
" 31. 28, "One *soul* (נֶפֶשׁ) of five hundred."
" 31. 35, "And thirty and two thousand *persons* (נֶפֶשׁ) in all." So also vs 40, 46.

Deut. 10. 22, "Threescore and ten *persons* (נֶפֶשׁ)."
" 24. 7, "If a man be found stealing *any* (נֶפֶשׁ, *a soul*) of his brethren"
" 27. 25, "Cursed be he that taketh reward to slay an innocent *person* (נֶפֶשׁ)"

Josh. 11. 11, "They smote all the *souls* (נֶפֶשׁ)." So in numerous other instances.

1 Sam. 22. 22, "I have occasioned the death of all the *persons* (נֶפֶשׁ) of thy father's house."

2 Sam. 14. 14, "Neither doth God respect any *person* (נֶפֶשׁ)."

Prov. 14. 25, "A true witness delivereth *souls* (נְפָשׁוֹת, i. e. *persons*)."
" 19. 15, "An idle *soul* (נֶפֶשׁ, i. e. *person*) shall suffer hunger)."

Jer. 43. 6, "Every *person* (נֶפֶשׁ) that Nebuzar-adan . . . had left"
" 52. 29, "Eight hundred thirty and two *persons* (נֶפֶשׁ)." So v. 30.

Ezek. 16. 5, "To the loathing of *thy person* (נַפְשֵׁךְ)."
" 17. 17, "To cut off many *persons* (נְפָשׁוֹת)."
" 22. 27, "To shed blood and to destroy *souls* (נְפָשׁוֹת, i e *persons*)."
" 27. 13, "They traded the *persons* (נֶפֶשׁ) of men." Comp. Rev. 18, 13.
" 33. 6, "If the sword come and take any *person* (נֶפֶשׁ) from among them."

Acts, 2. 41, "And the same day were added unto them about three thousand *souls* (ψυχαὶ)." So also ch. 7. 14—27, 37.

" 2. 43, "And fear came upon every *soul* (ψυχῇ)."

" 3 .23, "And it shall come to pass that every *soul* (ψυχὴ) which will not hear that prophet, shall be destroyed."

Rom. 2. 9, "Tribulation and anguish upon every *soul* (ψυχὴν) of man that doeth evil."

1 Cor. 15. 45, "The first Adam was made *a living soul* (εἰς ψυχὴν ζῶσαν), the last Adam was made *a quickening spirit* (εἰς πνεῦμα ζωοποιοῦν)."

The peculiarity in this passage is so striking as to deserve especial remark. The allusion is direct and verbal to Gen. 2. 7, as rendered in the Greek of the Septuagint, "And the Lord God formed man of the dust of the ground, and breathed into his nostrils the breath of life, and he became *a living soul* (εἰς ψυχὴν ζῶσαν)." The question arises as to the precise point of the contrast between the two Adams. The solution would be less difficult if we could fully satisfy ourselves on another question, viz., whether the designations were strictly intended to be *personal* or *collective*—whether by the "first Adam," was meant exclusively the individual progenitor of our race, and by the "last Adam," Christ; or whether "Adam" in both cases is a generic term for *man*, the first denoting *man* as fallen, sinful, earthly; the second, *man* as regenerated, spiritual, heavenly. This latter view we think may be admitted, while we admit at the same time that *man*, in this twofold character, is *represented* by the two persons thus denominated. It is certain that the name "Adam" is applied as a title of the *collective humanity* of the race in its fallen state, as when it is said, Gen. 6. 5, that "God saw the wickedness of *man* (הָאָדָם *the Adam*), that it was great." (Comp. Gen. 1. 26, 27; 5. 1; 6. 1.) It is in this sense analogous to the "old man" which is to be put off in order that the "new man," which Christ represents, may be put on. If this be not the import here, it is extremely difficult to discover the justness of the ground on which the apostle asserts of Adam individually that he was made εἰς ψυχὴν ζῶσαν, *a living soul*, viewing the term ψυχή as the opposite to πνεῦμα, *spirit;* for if Adam was created *holy*, as is universally conceded, it would seem that he must have been πνευματικός, *spiritual*, as well as ψυχικός, *psychical* or *natural*. Yet the quotation literally taken refers to Adam at his first creation, and before his fall. He was then, it is true, created a ψυχὴ ζῶσα, *a living soul*, but this could not of itself set him in opposition to Christ considered as πνευματικός, *spiritual*, because he also by being *holy* must have been *spiritual*, nor does any one of the saints by becoming *spiritual* cease thereby to be *psychical* in the sense of which ψυχή is affirmed of Adam at his creation. How then can a contrast be made out between the *psychical body* of unfallen Adam and the *spiritual body* of the resurrection, which is held to be derived from the quickening virtue of Christ the Lord?

The use of a term denoting simply *natural* or *animal life* does not of itself contradistinguish the body here inhabited by regenerate man from the *spiritual* or *resurrection* body, because the *animal* or *psychical* principle does not become extinct in consequence of a man's being rendered *spiritual* by virtue of his union to Christ. How then, we ask again, is the contrast established between sinless Adam as a ψυχή and Christ as a πνεῦμα? We are for ourselves unable to answer the question but upon the view above suggested, that Adam is here to be understood *generically*, and that the phrase ψυχὴ ζῶσα is to be taken as a predicate of *fallen humanity*, in which the *psychical* principle, viewed as the seat of sensation, temptation, concupiscence, and the various forms of sinful and corrupt affection, has obtained the ascendency. The "first man Adam," therefore, we take to be a designation of the *first collective man* in his lapsed and sinful state prior to his becoming morally renewed, and thus capable of having his *psychical* body *spiritualized* by coming under the transforming influence of the Spirit of Christ. He is in that state *psychical* in a bad sense just as he is *fleshly* in a bad sense. But as a Christian does not by being regenerated cease to be possessed of *flesh* as a constituent element of his nature, so neither does he cease, from the same cause, to be possessed of a $\psi v \chi \dot{\eta}$ by means of which he passes into the other world in a *psychical* body.

It is a fact, indeed, that the apostle quotes an expression which is applied in the original reference to the personal Adam at his creation, but the whole drift of his discourse makes it evident that it is to be understood as a predicate of his fallen descendants in their natural or unrenewed state, in which the *psychical* or *sensual* nature has obtained such a paramount sway as properly to denominate the whole man. This construction brings the entire context into harmony. "It is sown a *natural body* ($\sigma \tilde{\omega} \mu a \ \psi v \chi \iota \varkappa \acute{o} v$), it is raised a *spiritual body* ($\sigma \tilde{\omega} \mu a \ \pi v \epsilon v \mu a \tau \iota \varkappa \grave{o} v$)." That is, it is sown a natural or psychical body, not at its burial after death, but *in its origin* as derived from a mainly psychical source, for "that which is born of the flesh, is flesh," as "that which is born of the Spirit, is spirit." Man is sown a natural body by his birth from a natural, i. e. a sinful, parentage. He then adds, "There is a natural body, and there is a spiritual body," and this he goes on to illustrate, rather than prove, by the above quotation from Genesis, in which he applies the language originally spoken of Adam as an individual before his fall to the collective race of Adam after the fall, in order to indicate the character of the change which it would be requisite for them to undergo that they might become partakers of a resurrection which should put them in possession of *spiritual* bodies, i. e. bodies brought under the controlling influence of the divine Spirit, as the former were under the prevailing dominion of the sensual *psyche*. "And so it is written, The first man Adam (i. e. man collectively in his first or fallen state, known in Scripture by the generic title 'Adam') was made a living soul; the last Adam was made a quickening spirit. Howbeit, that was not first which is spiritual, but that which is natural; and afterward that which is spiritual." That is, the fallen or dominantly *psychical* humanity was prior in order to the *spiritual* or regenerate. "The first man (the first collective fallen man, who may be conceived as embodied and represented in the person of Adam) is of the earth, earthy; the second man (in like manner embodied and represented in Christ) is the Lord from heaven " Here it is remarkable that the word "Lord" ($κύριος$) is wanting in some early copies of high repute, which has induced Lachman to leave it out of the text of his edition of the New Testament, and it is wanting also in the Latin Vulgate, which renders, "Secundus homo de cœlo, cœlestis," *the second man from heaven (is) heavenly;* or *the second man (is) from heaven, heavenly."* Now though we cannot doubt that Christ is here really alluded to, as Adam is in the previous clause, yet we conceive the true idea is that of a collective body of whom Christ is to be regarded as the representative type, and we cannot but deem the internal evidence of the passage *against* the reading which inserts "Lord." The conformity of the two collective bodies to their representing heads is clearly developed in the ensuing verse; "As is the earthy, such are they also that are earthy; and as is the heavenly, such are they also that are heavenly."

It will be observed that the scope of the apostle is all along to illustrate the doctrine of the resurrection, and to show how the resurrection-body is distinguished from the natural body. With this view he presents Adam and Christ, the respective representatives of each, in strong contrast with each other. But it is fallen, or predominantly *psychical* Adam, that is set before us, and while he is called a *living soul,* Christ is called a *quickening spirit.* The term *quickening* in this connexion is usually understood as equivalent to *life-giving* or *life-imparting;* and as the resurrection is the particular theme of discourse, it is supposed that the term points to that divine power by which Christ raises the bodies of his people from the dead and endows them with resurrection-life. But if the resurrection set forth in this chapter be the resurrection of the *bodies* of the saints, it would seem that this would depend rather upon the exertion of what we may term *physical* than of *spiritual* omnipotence, for it is not easy to perceive how the divine *spiritual* agency should act upon any thing but the *spiritual* nature of man. As then the epithet ζωοποιοῦν, *quickening*, has no object expressed upon which the action can be supposed to fall, we take it as intended to denote the vivifying power which is put forth not upon the *dead bodies*, but upon the *dead spirits*, of men, raising them up by regeneration to a new spiritual life, which receives its consummation in the resurrection upon which they enter at death. It is scarcely possible, we think, to overlook the fact, that not only here, but throughout the New Testament, the resurrection of the saints is spoken of but as the completed issue of their regeneration. It is not represented as a great event suspended upon the exertion of the same kind of power with that which called the universe into being, but rather as the normal and necessary result of that divine operative energy by which they are first awakened from the death of trespasses and sins and made new creatures in Christ Jesus. Thus Paul, in so earnestly desiring and pressing on to attain the resurrection of the dead, is but breathing after the completed result of his regeneration, which he expresses by "apprehending that for which he also is apprehended of Christ."

Adopting this interpretation we may still retain the *collective* sense which we have affirmed of the two Adams. As the "first man," viewed as corrupt and fallen, was made a *living soul*, or one in which the *psychical* nature predominated, so the "second man," of which Christ is the head, was made a *quickening*, i. e. a *self-quickening spirit*. The power which wrought in him and so gloriously demonstrated itself in his resurrection from the dead, works also in them to the same result, and though flowing from him as its source, yet it eventuates in presenting the whole sanctified and transmuted body, both head and members, as a self-quickened spirit, where *spirit* doubtless has the sense of a *spiritual person*, just as *living soul* denotes a *person*. And that this term, in reference to Christ himself, has truly such an import and points to his *resurrection-person*, is evinced, we think, by the following passages. Rom. 1. 3, 4, "Concerning his Son Jesus Christ our Lord, which was made of the seed of David according to the flesh (κατὰ σάρκα), and declared to be the Son of God with power *according to the spirit of holiness* (κατὰ πνεῦμα ἁγιοσύνης) by the resurrection from the dead." Here it is evident that the phrases "according to the flesh" and "according to the spirit of holiness" (i.e. holy spirit, by which, however, is not meant the third person of the Trinity), are set in designed contrast with each other, the one denoting his fleshly human nature prior to the resurrection, the other his exalted spiritual nature subsequent to that event. The term πνεῦμα plainly imports that condition or state into which he came by his resurrection from the dead, and which could never have been affirmed of the simple resuscitation of his entombed fleshly body. It is in fact the designation of his raised, spiritual, and glorified body, and in the same sense is it to be understood in the passage under consideration, where the same exalted personage is called a *quickening spirit*. Thus, too, 1 Tim. 3. 16, "God was manifest in the flesh, *justified in the spirit* (ἐδικαιώθη ἐν πνεύματι), seen of angels, preached unto the Gentiles, believed on in the world, received up into glory." This is a compendious summary of the entire process through which the divine Redeemer passed from his birth to his ascension to heaven. The clause, "justified in the spirit," where the original (ἐν πνεύματι) lacks the article, showing that it cannot mean that he was justified *by the Holy Spirit*, refers to his resurrection. He was justified, i. e. publicly acknowledged and accredited, as the true

Messiah, by being translated at his resurrection into a *spiritual* state and form, as gloriously distinguished from his previous fleshly mode of manifestation. So also 1 Pet. 3. 18, "Christ also hath once suffered for sins, the just for the unjust, that he might bring us to God, being put to death *in the flesh* (σαρχί), but quickened *by the spirit* (πνεύματι)." Here again we recognize a contrast in the ante- and the post-resurrection state of Christ, the one denoted by σαρξ, *flesh*, and the other by πνεῦμα, *spirit*. In both, as in the previous instances, allusion is had to his twofold body, the one of his humiliation, the other of his glorification. The one is *fleshly*, the other is *spiritual*. If his material body had been raised unchanged, he would have been *quickened in the flesh*, which he certainly was not. He was quickened in a spiritual body as truly as he was put to death in a material body, and this is indicated by the original terms σαρχί and πνεύματι, which are grammatically parallel with each other.

From all that has now been adduced we find the light of a strong illustration thrown upon the words of the apostle in the passage under review. "The last Adam was made a quickening spirit." The language points directly to Christ *in his resurrection-state* as the exemplar of the saints when they also shall have assumed their resurrection-bodies. It is in this that the true antithesis lies between the two mystic Adams, the state of the one being predominantly *psychical*, in the sense of fallen, sinful, sensual; the other possessed of a nature *spiritual*, i e sanctified, celestial, glorious And such as the *state* is, such also is the *body* appropriated to each. For ourselves we can scarcely conceive of any evidence more decisive that our Lord arose in a *spiritual* instead of a *fleshly* body, and that his resurrection-state during the forty days previous to the ascension was an express prototype of the *spiritual* bodies which the saints, like their great pattern, assume, when they like him pass from these bodies of clay into their immortal corporeity.

In some few of the above citations it may be doubtful whether the idea of *lives* is not more legitimately the sense of *souls*, but as to the mass of them there can be no question but that they are rightly represented by the word *persons*.

We now come to a class, very closely related to the preceding, where the word stands for that which constitutes the *conscious inner and essential self* of man, without however affording any clew to the *intrinsic nature or properties of the substance* to which it refers. It is a usage grounded upon the universally innate impression that *a man's soul is, par eminence, himself*.

§ 7.

נֶפֶשׁ *in the sense of One's Self, or the interior and ground-element of his being, the Personal Hypostasis.*

Gen. 12. 13, "*My soul* (נפשׁי) shall live because of thee." That is, *I, myself*, shall live.
" 19 20, "Let me escape thither, and *my soul* (נפשׁי) shall live " That is, *I* shall live
" 27. 4, "That *my soul* (נפשׁי) may bless thee." That is, that *I* may bless thee. So also vs 19, 25, 31.
" 49. 6, " *O my soul* (נפשׁי), come not thou into their secret." That is, *O myself*, come not.
Ex. 30. 15, " To make an atonement for *your souls* (נַפְשֹׁתֵיכֶם)." That is, for *yourselves*. And so in innumerable other cases.
Lev. 11. 43, "Ye shall not make *yourselves* (נַפְשֹׁתֵיכֶם, marg. *your souls*) abominable."
" 11. 44, "Neither shall ye defile *yourselves* (נַפְשֹׁתֵיכֶם, *your souls*)."
Num. 16. 38, "The censers of these sinners against *their own souls* (בְּנַפְשֹׁתָם, i. e. *against themselves*) "
" 23. 10, "Let *me* (נפשׁי, *my soul*) die the death of the righteous."

USAGE OF נֶפֶשׁ, ψυχή, SOUL, ETC.

Num. 30. 2, "To bind *his soul* (נַפְשׁוֹ, i. e. *himself*) with a bond." So also vs. 4—11.

Deut. 4. 15, "Take ye therefore good heed unto *yourselves* (נַפְשֹׁתֵיכֶם, *your souls*)."

Judg. 5. 21, "*O my soul* (נַפְשִׁי), thou hast trodden down strength."

" 16. 30, "Let *me* (נַפְשִׁי, *my soul*) die with the Philistines."

1 Sam. 1. 15, "But have poured out *my soul* (נַפְשִׁי) before the Lord," i. e. have unbosomed myself, have laid open my inmost thoughts and feelings.

" 25. 26, "As *thy soul* (נַפְשְׁךָ) liveth," i. e. as *thou thyself* livest.

1 Kings, 1. 29, "That hath redeemed *my soul* (נַפְשִׁי)," i. e. hath redeemed *me*, *myself*.

Est. 4. 13, "Think not with *thyself* (נַפְשֵׁךְ, *thy soul*) that thou shalt escape."

" 9. 31, "As they had decreed for *themselves* (נַפְשָׁם, *their souls*)."

Job, 7. 15, "*My soul* (נַפְשִׁי) chooseth strangling," i. e. *I* choose.

" 9. 21, "Yet would I not know *my soul* (נַפְשִׁי)," i. e. would not approve *myself*.

" 16. 4, "If *your soul* (נַפְשְׁכֶם) were in *my soul's* (נַפְשִׁי) stead," i. e. if *you* were in *my* stead.

" 31. 30, "Neither have I suffered my mouth to sin by wishing a curse to *his soul* (נַפְשׁוֹ)," i. e. to *him*.

" 32. 2, "Against Job was his wrath kindled because he justified *himself* (נַפְשׁוֹ *his soul*)"

" 33. 18, "He keepeth back *his soul* (נַפְשׁוֹ) from the pit," i. e. *him*. So also v. 30.

" 33. 22, "*His soul* (נַפְשׁוֹ) draweth near unto the grave," i. e. *he* draws near; or we may understand it of his *life*.

Ps. 3. 2, "Many there be which say of *my soul* (נַפְשִׁי)," i. e. of *me*.

Ps. 7. 2, "Lest he tear *my soul* (נַפְשִׁי) like a lion," i. e. tear *me*.

" 7. 5, " Let the enemy persecute *my soul* (נַפְשִׁי)," i. e. *me*.

" 11. 1, " How say ye to *my soul* (נַפְשִׁי)," i. e. to *me*.

" 13. 2, " Shall I take counsel in *my soul* (נַפְשִׁי)," i. e. with *myself*.

" 16. 10, " Thou wilt not leave *my soul* (נַפְשִׁי) in hell," i. e. wilt not leave *me*. So also as quoted Acts 2 27, 31.

" 17. 13, " Deliver *my soul* (נַפְשִׁי) from the wicked," i e. deliver *me*. So 22. 10.

" 22. 29, " None can keep alive *his own soul* (נַפְשׁוֹ)," i. e. *himself*.

" 25. 13, " *His soul* (נַפְשׁוֹ) shall dwell at ease," i. e. *he* shall dwell.

" 26. 9, " Gather not *my soul* (נַפְשִׁי) with sinners," i. e. *me*.

" 31. 7, " Thou hast known *my soul* (נַפְשִׁי) in adversities," i. e. *me*.

" 35. 17, " Rescue *my soul* (נַפְשִׁי) from their destructions," i. e. *me*.

" 42. 5, 11, "Why art thou cast down, *O my soul*, (נַפְשִׁי)," i. e. *O myself*.

" 49. 18, " Though he blessed *his soul* (נַפְשׁוֹ)," i e. *himself*.

" 66. 16, " I will declare what he hath done for *my soul* (נַפְשִׁי)," i. e. for *me*.

" 105. 18, " *He* (נַפְשׁוֹ, *his soul*) was laid in iron.

" 109. 20, " Them that speak evil against *my soul* (נַפְשִׁי)," i. e. against *me*.

" 119. 67, " *My soul* (נַפְשִׁי) hath kept thy testimonies," i. e. *I* have kept.

" 131. 2, " I have behaved and quieted *myself* (נַפְשִׁי, *my soul*)."

Ps. 139 14, "And that *my soul* (נַפְשִׁי) knoweth right well," i. e. *I* know.

Prov. 16 26, "*He* (נֶפֶשׁ, *the soul)* that laboreth, laboreth for himself."

Is. 5 14, "Therefore hell hath enlarged *herself* (נַפְשָׁהּ *her soul)*" Figuratively spoken.

" 44. 20, "A deceived heart hath turned him aside, that he cannot deliver *his soul* (נַפְשׁוֹ)," i. e. *himself*.

" 46. 2, "They could not deliver the burden, but *themselves* (נַפְשָׁם, *their souls*) are gone into captivity."

" 47 14, "They shall not deliver *themselves* (נַפְשָׁם, *their souls*)."

" 51. 23, "Which have said to *thy soul* (נַפְשֵׁךְ), bow down;" i e which have said to *thee*.

Jer. 3. 11, "The backsliding Israel hath justified *herself* (נַפְשָׁהּ, *her soul*)."

" 17. 21, "Take heed to *yourselves* (בְּנַפְשׁוֹתֵיכֶם), to *your souls*)."

" 37 9, "Deceive not *yourselves* (נַפְשֹׁתֵכֶם, *your souls*)"

" 40 15, "Wherefore should he slay *thee* (נֶפֶשׁ, *thy soul*)?"

Ezek. 4 14, "*My soul* (נֶפֶשׁ) hath not been polluted"

" 33. 5, "He that taketh warning shall deliver *his soul* (נַפְשׁוֹ)," i e. *himself*

Am. 2 14, "Neither shall the mighty deliver *himself* (נַפְשׁוֹ, *his soul*)." So v. 15.

Jon. 4. 8, "He wished in *himself* (נַפְשׁוֹ, *his soul*) to die."

Luke, 1. 46, "My *soul* (ψυχή) doth magnify the Lord," i. e. *I* do magnify.

" 21. 19, "In patience possess ye your *souls* (ψυχάς)," i e. possess *yourselves*.

Rom. 13, 1, "Let every *soul* (ψυχή) be subject to the higher powers."

2 Cor 12. 15, "I will very gladly spend and be spent *for you* (ὑπὲρ τῶν ψυχῶν ὑμῶν, *for your souls*)."

1 Thes 2 8, "We were willing to have imparted unto

you, not the gospel of God only, but also our own *souls* (ψυχὰς)," i. e. *ourselves*.

James, 1. 21, " Receive with meekness the ingrafted word, which is able to save your *souls* (ψυχὰς)."

" 5. 20, " He which converteth a sinner from the error of his way shall save a *soul* (ψυχὴν) from death."

2 Pet. 2, 14, " Beguiling unstable *souls* (ψυχὰς)."

Rev. 16. 3, " And every living *soul* (ψυχὴ) died in the sea."

There undoubtedly remains uncited a numerous list of passages under this head, which is perhaps more extensive than any other. But all the prominent passages are given, and their purport is very obvious. They recognize the fact, that man is man *from his soul,* or as Cicero says, *Mens cujusque is quisque, every man's mind is himself.* It is that part of his nature which gives denomination to the whole. At the same time this usage affords no clew to the essential and ontological properties of this element of his being. We are left to determine this, if possible, from our own researches in the field of physiology and psychology. The Scriptures speak on the subject from the *communis sensus* of the whole human race. Every one knows that he has an inner principle of life, thought, sensation, and action, apart from his bodily structure, and all languages proceed on the principle of predicating of this interior element those attributes which distinguish the *man* as a compound entity consisting of *soul* and *body.* The Scriptures evidently profess nothing more.

In the list of texts above displayed the reader will be struck with several in which the *soul* is said to *die* as well as to *live.* Thus, Judges, 16. 30, " *Let me die* (נַפְשִׁי תָּמוֹת, *let my soul die*) with the Philistines." Num. 23. 10, " *Let me die* (תָּמֹת נַפְשִׁי) the death of the righteous." Job. 36. 14, " *They die* (תָּמֹת נַפְשָׁם *their soul dieth*) in youth, and their life is among the unclean." Probably nothing more is intimated by this than the *cessation of life,* yet the phraseology is remarkable when viewed in connexion with our ordinary ideas of the meaning of the word *soul* as indicating that principle of our being which is regarded in its own nature as immortal.

We give in this connexion the several passages in which the term is applied to God.

Lev. 26, 11, "And I will set my tabernacle amongst you; and *my soul* (נפשי) shall not abhor you." So v. 30.

Judg. 10. 16, "And they put away the strange gods from among them, and served the Lord: and *his soul* (נפשו) was grieved for the misery of Israel."

Is 1. 14, "Your appointed feasts *my soul* (נפשי) hateth."

Jer. 5. 9, 29, "Shall not *my soul* (נפשי) be avenged on such a nation as this?" So also ch. 9. 9.

" 6. 8, "Be then instructed, O Jerusalem, lest *my soul* (נפשי) depart from thee."

" 12. 7, "I have given the dearly beloved of *my soul* (נפשי) into the hand of her enemies."

" 14. 19, "Hast thou utterly rejected Judah? hath *thy soul* (נפשך) loathed Zion?"

" 15. 1, "Though Moses and Samuel stood before me, yet *my mind* (נפשי, *my soul*) could not be toward this people."

" 32. 41, "I will plant them in this land assuredly with my whole *heart* and with *my* whole *soul* (נפשי)."

" 51. 14, "The Lord of hosts hath sworn by *himself* (נפשו, *his soul*)."

Ezek. 23. 18, "Then *my mind* (נפשי, *my soul*) was alienated from her."

Am. 6. 8, "The Lord God hath sworn by *himself* (נפשו, *his soul*)"

Zech. 11. 8, "And *my soul* (נפשי) loathed them, and their soul also abhorred me."

In the following texts we find the term applied to Christ.

Ps. 16. 10, "Thou wilt not leave *my soul* (נפשי) in hell, nor suffer thine holy one to see corruption."

Is. 53. 10, "When thou shalt make *his soul* (נַפְשׁוֹ) an offering for sin."

" 53 11, "He shall see of the travail of *his soul* (נַפְשׁוֹ), and be satisfied"

" 53. 12, "Because he hath poured out *his soul* (נַפְשׁוֹ) unto death"

§ 8.

נֶפֶשׁ *in the sense of Dead Body.*

We come now to a very peculiar usage by which נֶפֶשׁ, as well as its Greek representative ψυχή, is applied to a *dead body* It is probable that in the cases coming under this head the phrase is elliptical, the full formula being נֶפֶשׁ מֵת, *soul or life of a dead person, or corpse,* which, as will be seen, occurs in two or three instances It is true that even in this sense the expression is somewhat singular, but it finds an analogy in that form of speech by which the *widow* of a deceased person is still called his *wife* Thus, Gen 38. 8, "And Judah said unto Onan, Go in unto thy brother's *wife* (widow), and marry her, and raise up seed to thy brother." Deut. 25. 5, "The *wife* of the dead shall not marry a stranger." V 7, "And if the man like not to take his brother's *wife*, then let his brother's *wife* go to the gate unto the elders, and say," &c In like manner, the soul *had been* the consort of the body, as the wife of the husband, and though it is true that the visible *relic* in this case is the *body* instead of the *soul*, yet it is doing no special violence to language to apply to that *relic* the term by which its higher and nobler part had been in life distinguished If this be not the true solution of a singular philological problem, we leave it to the decision of some more sagacious investigator Gesenius and Winer, however, maintain that there is an ellipsis of מֵת, *corpse.*

Lev 19. 28, "Ye shall not make any cuttings in your flesh for the *dead* (נֶפֶשׁ)."

Lev. 21. 1, "There shall none be defiled for the *dead* (נפש) among his people."

" 21. 11, "Neither shall he go in to any *dead body* (נפשת מת lit. *souls of the dead*)."

" 22. 4, "Whoso toucheth any thing that is unclean by the *dead* (נפש)."

Num. 5. 2, "Every one that hath an issue, and whosoever is defiled by the *dead* (נפש)."

" '6. 6, "All the days that he separateth himself unto the Lord he shall come at no *dead body* (נפש מת, *soul of the dead*)."

" 6. 11, "For that he sinned by the *dead* (נפש)."

" 9 6, 7, "And there were certain men who were defiled by the *dead body* (נפש) of a man."

" 9. 10, "If any man of you shall be unclean by a *dead body* (נפש)."

" 19 13, "Whosoever toucheth the *dead body* (נפש) of any man."

Hag. 2. 13, "If one that is unclean by a *dead body* (נפש) touch any of these, shall it be unclean?"

We have thus arrayed before the eye of the reader the various scriptural usage which obtains in regard to the word נפש=ψυχή=*soul*. We have seen that in its first and lowest sense, as conveyed by its etymology, it denotes the *breath*, and thence by natural transition the *life*, the presence of which is most obviously indicated by the act of *respiration*. But as *life* in the animal world is not found apart from *sensation*, therefore, as might be expected, the term which is used to denote the principle of *life* naturally extends itself to designate the principle which is the immediate seat and subject of *sensation*. Up to this point, however, we recognize nothing in the import of the term which does not apply to the brute creation as well as to man, for brutes *live* and *feel*, as truly as do men; and so far as the word *soul* expresses simply *life* and *sensation*, so far the beasts are possessed of *souls* as well as men. But the word is used in a yet higher sense Where we find *sensation* we find *senses* and *sensual* appetites and desires—certain inbred promptings which refer themselves more especially to the *body*, because, in the present life, we can only recognize these senses as a part of the bodily economy. Still as the body is entirely devoid of these sensations when forsaken of the soul, we naturally infer that the sentient power is strictly an attribute of the *soul* and not of the *body;* nor can we well resist the inference that this power goes forth with the soul into the new sphere to which it is transferred at death, although there necessarily acted upon and exercised by different objects from those with which it was conversant in the life of the body. In the definite conception of this change we are aided by the analogies drawn from the insect world. The sentient power of the caterpillar doubtless passes with its life into the butterfly form, but it is there acted upon by entirely different objects from those which excited its sensitivity in its primitive structure. It is now a denizen of the atmosphere, refreshed by its aromas, and looking upon scenes new and strange to its tiny eyes, but still with its sensitive nature not only perfectly retained, but vastly improved. So with man subsequent to his translation into the spiritual world.

Advancing still farther in the gradation of sense, we find the term extending its import to embrace the idea of a higher class of *affections* such as pertain mostly to a rational being, and imply the exercise of those various *passions* and *emotions* which have their seat in a higher region of intellect. The examples however of this usage, given under the fourth head, evince that we are still within the range of that import of the word which applies to beasts as well as to man. Nothing is more obvious than that the brute creation is possessed of *emotions* and *passions* as truly as man. While the degree of *intelligence* they manifest is often astonishing, they give proof also of being affected by *love, joy, fear, sor-*

row, hatred, jealousy, and *shame* So far therefore as these affections in man can be predicated of the ψυχή, or *soul*, as their subject, so far must they be referred to the same subject in the nature of beasts Still man is distinguished by a heaven-wide difference from the highest grade of the brute tribes, yet not upon the ground of the ψυχή. The basis of the distinction is laid in man's possession of the πνεῦμα, or *spirit*, which, as we shall see, is never truly predicated of the beasts of the field.

But waiving this for the present, we remark, that the next and most important sense of the term is that of *person*. It is perfectly obvious, from the multitudinous instances adduced, that *the soul is but a denomination for the man*, and the inference is not only legitimate, but inevitable, that man exists in the most absolute integrity of his nature, apart from the material body which he here inhabits, for nothing is clearer than that the term ψυχή is applied to man after his dislodgment from the house of clay. Thus, Rev. 6. 9, "And when he had opened the fifth seal, I saw under the altar the *souls* (ψυχάς) of them that were slain," &c. Ch 20. 4, " And I saw the *souls* (ψυχάς) of them that were beheaded for the witness of Jesus." So Wisd. 3. 1, "The *souls* (ψυχαί) of the just are in the hands of God." But upon this idea we shall dwell more at length in a subsequent page. We now purpose to investigate the usage in relation to the original words for *spirit*.

CHAPTER III.

Import of Original Scriptural Terms for Spirit.

§ 1.

רוּחַ (*ruahh*), πνεῦμα (*pneuma*), *Spirit*.

This is one of those terms in Hebrew which it is impossible, on satisfactory grounds, to refer to any verbal root more primitive than itself. The Lexicons exhibit, indeed, the cognate word רָוַח *rávahh, to breathe,* or rather *to breathe freely,* by which the breast is enlarged, dilated, and refreshed, and thence giving the natural secondary sense of *large, ample, spacious,* as may be seen by consulting 1 Sam 16. 23, "*So Saul was refreshed* (וְרָוַח שָׁאוּל—Lit. *and refreshing was to Saul.*)" Job, 32. 20, "I will speak *that I may be refreshed* (וְיִרְוַח לִי—Lit. *and refreshment shall be to me*)." Jer. 22. 14, "I will build me a wide house and *large* (מְרֻוָּחִים *spacious, airy*) chambers." So with the derivatives רֶוַח *revahh* and רְוָחָה *revâhhâh;* Est. 4. 14, "If thou altogether holdest thy peace at this time, then shall there *enlargement* (רֶוַח *revahh*) and deliverance arise to the Jews from another place" Gen 32 14, "And put a *space* (רֶוַח *revahh*) between drove and drove," i. e. a free space, an ample interval, the opposite of strait, or constrained. Ex. 8. 15, "But when Pharaoh saw that there was *respite* (רְוָחָה, *a breathing-spell*), he hardened his heart." Lam. 3. 56, "Hide not thine ear at *my breathing* (רַוְחָתִי)." We have also the supposititious verbal רוּחַ *ruahh* in the sense of *breathing* or *blowing,* but it nowhere occurs in the Kal or simplest form, but only in Hiphil or the causative form (הֵרִיחַ *hērıahh*), and there with the import of *smelling,* the relation of which to the *breathing process* is quite obvious. But even this verb is undoubtedly a denominative from the noun רִיחַ *riahh, scent, smell,* just as הִנְפִּישׁ is from נֶפֶשׁ Yet that there is a mutual relation between the forms רָוַח, רִיחַ, and רוּחַ, is unquestionable from the fact that the radical idea of *breath, air in motion, air inhaled and exhaled,* is fundamental to each of them; but we know of no competent authority for making the verb רָוַח the primitive root, any more than רוּחַ or רִיחַ. The idea of air in the form of *breath* or *wind* is doubtless of as early origin as that of the *act* by which it is put in motion, and which would be expressed by a verb. Assuming then the principle, which is generally adopted by lexicographers, that the *physical* idea of most words is primitive, we may assign *breath* as the first sense of רוּחַ, and *wind* as the second. From these the subordinate tropical applications of the term will be seen to flow by a very natural train of sequence.

The corresponding Greek term πνεῦμα comes from πνέω, *to blow*, and thus affords another instance of the etymological relation of this class of words to roots having reference to *air* or *wind*. Like the Heb. original this term also occurs in the lower or physical sense of *wind* and *breath*, as Gen. 8. 1, "And God made a *wind* (πνεῦμα) to pass over the earth." Eccl. 1. 6, "The *wind* (πνεῦμα) goeth toward the south, and turneth about unto the north." Is. 7. 2, "And his heart was moved and the heart of his people, as the trees of the wood are moved *by the wind* (ὑπὸ πνεύματος)." Ps 135. 17, "They have ears but they hear not; neither is there any *breath* (πνεῦμα) in their mouths." John, 3. 8, "The *wind* (πνεῦμα) bloweth where it listeth, and thou hearest the sound thereof," &c In ordinary usage, however, it denotes, like its Heb. equivalent, the *spirit* of God or man in one or other of the various senses disclosed under the ensuing list of citations, the result of which it will not be necessary here to anticipate

§ 2.

(1.) רוּחַ *in the sense of Breath.*

1. *Spoken of man.*

Gen. 6 17, "All flesh wherein is the *breath of life* (רִיחַ חַיִּים)." So also ch. 7. 15.

" 7. 22, "All in whose nostrils was the *breath of life* (רוּחַ חַיִּים)—Marg. the breath of *the spirit of life*)."

Job, 9. 18, "He will not suffer me to take *my breath* (רוּחִי)."

" 12. 10, "In whose hand is the soul of every living thing, and the *breath* (רוּחַ) of all mankind."

" 15 30, "By the *breath* (רוּחַ) of his mouth shall he go away."

Job, 17. 1, "*My breath* (רוחי) is corrupt, my days are extinct, the graves are ready for me."

" 19. 17, "*My breath* (רוחי) is strange to my wife."

" 27. 3, "All the while my breath is in me, and the *spirit of God* (רוּחַ אֱלוֹהַ) is in my nostrils." That is, the spirit which God breathed into man at his creation The only instance in the Bible where "spirit of God" is used in this sense.

Ps. 135. 17, "They have ears but they hear not, neither is there any *breath* (רוּחַ) in their mouths."

" 146. 4, "His *breath* (רוּחוֹ) goeth forth, he returneth to his earth."

Eccl 3. 19, "Yea, they have all one *breath* (רוּחַ)."

Is. 33. 11, "*Your breath* (רוּחֲכֶם), as fire, shall devour you."

Jer. 10. 14, "His molten image is falsehood, and there is no *breath* (רוּחַ) in them." So also ch. 51. 17.

Lam. 4. 20, "The *breath* (רוּחַ) of our nostrils, the anointed of the Lord, was taken in their pits."

Ezek. 37. 5, "Behold, I will cause *breath* (רוּחַ) to enter into you, and ye shall live." Comp. v. 6, 8, 10.

Hab. 2. 19, "Behold, it is laid over with gold and silver, and there is no *breath* (רוּחַ) at all in the midst of it."

2. *Spoken of God.*

Ex. 15 8, "And with the *blast* (רוּחַ, *breath*) of thy nostrils the waters were gathered together."

2 Sam. 22. 16, "At the rebuking of the Lord, at the blast of the *breath* (רוּחַ) of his nostrils."

Job, 4. 9, "And by the *breath* (רוּחַ) of his nostrils are they consumed."

Ps. 18 15, "The foundations of the world were discovered . at the blast of the *breath* (רוּחַ) of thy nostrils"

" 33. 6, "By the word of the Lord were the heavens made; and all the host of them by the *breath* (רוּחַ) of his mouth."

Is. 11. 4, "And with the *breath* (רוּחַ) of his lips shall he slay the wicked."

Is. 30. 28, "And *his breath* (רוּחוֹת), as an overflowing stream, shall reach to the midst of the neck."

§ 3.

רוּחַ *in the sense of Wind,* Ἄνεμος.

1. *Simple air*—once only.

Job, 41, 16, "One is so near to another that no *air* (רוּחַ) can come between them."

2. *Common wind.*

Gen. 3. 8, "And they heard the voice of the Lord God walking in the garden *in the cool of the day* (לְרוּחַ הַיּוֹם, *in the cool or windy part of the day*)."

" 8. 1, "And God made a *wind* (רוּחַ) to pass over the earth."

Num. 11. 31, "The *wind* (רוּחַ) brought quails from the sea."

Ex. 10. 13, "The Lord brought an east *wind* (רוּחַ) upon the land . . . . and the east *wind* (רוּחַ) brought the locusts."

" 10. 19, "And the Lord turned a mighty strong west *wind* (רוּחַ), which took away the locusts." So also ch. 14. 21.

" 15. 10, "Thou didst blow with thy *wind* (רוּחַ), the sea covered them."

Num. 11. 31, "And there went forth a *wind* (רוּחַ) from the Lord, and brought quails from the sea."

2 Sam. 22, 11, "He was seen upon the wings of the *wind* (רוּחַ)."

1 Kings, 18. 45, "Heaven was black with clouds and *wind* (רוּחַ)."

" 19. 11, "And a great and strong *wind* (רוּחַ) rent the mountains." Comp. what follows.

3. *Violent wind or tempest.*

2 Kings, 19. 7, "Behold, I will send a *blast* (רוּחַ) upon him."

Ps. 11. 6, "Upon the wicked he shall rain snares, fire and brimstone, and an horrible *tempest* (רוּחַ)."

" 55. 8, "I would hasten my escape from the *windy storm* (רוּחַ) and tempest."

" 107. 25, "For he commandeth and raiseth the *stormy wind* (רוּחַ), which lifteth up the waves thereof."

" 148. 8, "Fire and hail; snow and vapor; *stormy wind* (רוּחַ) fulfilling his pleasure."

Is. 25. 4, "A shadow from the heat, when the *blast* (רוּחַ) of the terrible ones is as a storm against the wall."

Ezek. 1. 4, "And I looked, and behold, a *whirlwind* (רוּחַ) out of the north."

Hos. 13. 15, "The *wind of the Lord* (רוּחַ) shall come up," i. e. a great and violent wind.

4. *The four quarters of the heavens from which the winds blow; a side, or point of the compass.*

1 Chron. 9. 24, "In four *quarters* (רוּחוֹת) were the porters."

Ezek. 37. 9, "Come from the four *winds* (רוּחוֹת), O breath."

" 42. 16—20, "He measured the east *side* (רוּחַ, *wind*) . . . he measured the north *side* (רוּחַ) . . . he measured the south *side* (רוּחַ) . . . he turned about to the west *side* (רוּחַ) . . . he measured it by the four *sides* (רוּחוֹת)."

Dan. 8. 8, and 11. 4, "Toward the four *winds* (רוּחוֹת) of heaven."

Jer. 52. 23, "Ninety and six pomegranates on a *side* (רוּחַ, *wind*)."

Zech. 2. 6, "For I have spread you abroad as the four *winds* (רוּחוֹת) of the heaven, saith the Lord."

" 6. 5, "These are the four *spirits* (רוּחוֹת) of the heavens."

5. *As denoting windy, empty, vain.*

Job, 6. 26, "Do ye imagine to reprove words, and the speeches of one that is desperate, which are as the *wind* (רוּחַ)?"

Job, 15 2, "Should a wise man utter *vain knowledge* (דַּעַת רוּחַ *knowledge of wind*)?"

" 16 3, "Shall *vain words* (דברי רוח, *words of wind*) have an end?"

Prov. 11 29, "He that troubleth his own house shall inherit the *wind* (רוּחַ)."

Eccl 5. 16, "What profit hath he that hath labored *for the wind* (לָ־רוּחַ)?"

Is. 26 18, "We have been with child, we have been in pain, we have as it were brought forth *wind* (רוּחַ)"

" 41. 29, "Their molten images are *wind* (רוּחַ)"

Jer. 5. 13, "And the prophets shall become *wind* (רוּחַ)."

Hos. 8. 7, "For they have sown the *wind* (רוּחַ.)"

" 12 1, "Ephraim feedeth on *wind* (רוּחַ)."

Mic 2 11 "If a man walking in the *spirit* (רוּחַ) and falsehood do lie, saying," &c That is, with empty claims to being under the influence of the spirit

§ 4.

רוּחַ *in the sense of Anima*, ψυχή, *Animal Life, Vital Spirit, or the Principle of Life as embodied and manifested in the Breath of the Mouth and Nostrils.*

The term in this sense accords so strikingly in import with נפש, No 3, that, as applied to man, it is scarcely possible to draw a clear line of distinction between them There is this, however, to be observed in regard to them, that whereas נפש is spoken frequently of *beasts*, we find but a single instance, Eccl 3. 19, where רוּחַ occurs with that reference, and even there shall adduce evidence to show that it is so used in a rhetorical, instead of a literal sense. Nor can we positively affirm that several of the ensuing passages might not be more properly ranged either under the head of simple *breath* given above, or under that of *mind* or *rational spirit*, which follows The actual usage can alone enable the reader to judge.

Gen. 45. 27, "And when he saw the wagons which Joseph had sent to carry him, his *spirit revived* (וַתְּחִי רוּחוֹ)."

This denotes a revived and vigorous acting of the *vital principle*, which is generally indicated by a freer respiration, and which had been in a measure *deadened* by his previous grief. The literal rendering of the word for *revived* is *lived*. The *life* which had been comparatively *dormant* now *lived again*, as the *life* in Hebrew is frequently said to *live*.

Num. 16. 22, "O God, the God of the *spirits* (רוּחֹת) of all flesh." This may import no more than the *lives actuating all flesh*.

Judg. 15. 19, "And when he had drunk, *his spirit* (רוּחוֹ) came again, and he revived." His *vital energy* was restored.

1 Sam. 30. 12, "And when he had eaten, *his spirit* (רוּחוֹ) came again to him." Same as the preceding.

1 Kings, 10. 4, 5, "And when the queen of Sheba had seen all Solomon's wisdom, and the house which he had built, &c. . . . . there was no more *spirit* (רוּחַ) in her." There was a kind of failing or giving way of the *powers of life*. So also 2 Chron. 9. 4.

Job, 6. 4, "For the arrows of the Almighty are within me, the poison whereof drinketh up *my spirit* (רוּחִי)." Exhausts my life and strength. "Takes away my vigor, my comfort, my life." *Barnes.*

" 10. 12, "Thy visitation hath preserved *my spirit* (רוּחִי)." My life.

Ps. 31. 5, "Into thy hands I commit *my spirit* (רוּחִי)." My vital breath.

" 76. 12, "He shall cut off the *spirit* (רוּחַ) of princes; he is terrible to the kings of the earth." 'Spirit' here has doubtless the import of *life*.

Eccl. 8. 8, "No man hath power over the *spirit* (רוּחַ) to retain the *spirit* (רוּחַ), neither hath he power in the day of death." No man hath power over the *spirit of life*.

Eccl. 11. 5, "As thou knowest not the way of *spirit* (רוּחַ) nor how the bones do grow in the womb."

Here seems a designed contrast between the two constituent principles of man, the gross material body and the informing *life* or *spirit*.

Eccl. 12. 7, "Then shall the dust return to the earth as it was, and the *spirit* to God who gave it (רוּחַ)."

An allusion seems here intended to the original creation of man, when the body was first formed and the *spirit* or *life* breathed into it. This body is to be decomposed again into its original elements, and the *informing life* restored to the great Being who first imparted it. The amount of implication of *mental faculties* seems to be the same in both cases. Still we would not contend with any one who should hold that *spirit* in this passage is to be distinctly understood of the *rational principle*, more especially than of the *vital*. The two senses run so nearly into each other that it is difficult to discriminate them.

Is. 38 16, "By these things men live, and in all these things is the *life of my spirit* (הַיֵּי רוּחִי)." That is, *my life*, says Gesenius.

" 42. 5, "He that giveth breath unto the people, and *spirit* (רוּחַ) to them that walk therein." That giveth *life*.

Mat. 27 50, "Jesus when he had cried again with a loud voice, yielded up the *ghost* (πνεῦμα)."

Luke, 8. 55, "And her *spirit* (πνεῦμα) came again, and she arose straightway."

§ 5.

רוּחַ *in the sense of Animus, Πνεῦμα, Spirit, the Mind, viewed as the Seat and Subject of Thought, but more especially of Emotion, Feeling, Passion, and Affection.*

Under the present head is to be classed an extended catalogue of passages in which, while we recognize a general community of import, we detect also various minor shades of difference that render an accurate discrimination extremely difficult. Of the two we think there can be little doubt that the term רוּחַ is intended to represent a higher element in our being than נֶפֶשׁ, though in many cases it will be found scarcely possible to distinguish their import. The dominant idea conveyed by רוּחַ, in its psychical relations, we believe to be that of *feeling*, of *emotion*, rather than of *thought* or *intellection*, though that is included. But we shall look in vain for any intimation of the intrinsic *nature* of that substance which thus *thinks* and *feels*—a point which we are left to determine, if practicable, by the lights of our own intelligence. The passage which comes the nearest to a scientific enunciation on this head, as already intimated, is Is. 31. 3, "Their horses are flesh, and not *spirit* (רוּחַ)," which certainly conveys the idea of a marked contrariety in the *essential nature* of the two subjects, without at the same time positively affirming in what it consists. In all other cases the term is employed exclusively with a moral or practical import, and recognizes only the common notions, which were not founded, in the minds of the Hebrews, upon any precise or scientific views of the true psychology of our being. Nothing more is assumed than that mankind are universally conscious of being possessed of certain *feelings* and *promptings* which in many cases refer themselves to a *divine* source, as is evident from the fact, that the operations of man's *spirit* are often ascribed to the influences of God's *spirit*. It is represented as being mainly through the medium of his *spirit* that man comes into conjunction with the Deity, the same term being applied to both.

A very frequent usage of the term is an adjunct to certain words expressive of various kinds of emotion, temper, or disposition, as a *spirit* of love, of hatred, of wisdom, of jealousy, of pride, of anger, of grief, of counsel, of adoption, of divination, of bondage, of burning, of error, of infirmity, of slumber, of judgment, of knowledge, &c., of which numerous instances are given below. Cases also occur in which a *spirit* is said to be taken from one and made to pass to another, as the *spirit* of *prophecy*.

(1) *Spoken of man and of Christ.*

Gen. 26. 35, " Which were a *grief of mind* (מֹרַת רוּחַ) unto Isaac and to Rebecca."

" 41. 8, " And it came to pass in the morning that *his spirit* (רוּחוֹ) was troubled."

Ex. 6. 9, " They hearkened not unto Moses for anguish of *spirit* (רוּחַ) "

Num. 11. 17, " I will take of the *spirit* (רוּחַ) which is upon thee and will put it upon them."

" 2. 5, " And the Lord took of the *spirit* (רוּחַ) that was upon him, and gave it unto the seventy elders; and it came to pass that when the *spirit* (רוּחַ) rested upon them, they prophesied."

" 14. 24, " But my servant Caleb, because he had another *spirit* (רוּחַ) with him."

Deut. 2. 30. " The Lord God hardened *his spirit* (רוּחוֹ)."

Josh. 2. 11, " As soon as we had heard these things, our hearts did melt, neither did there remain any more *courage* (רוּחַ, *spirit*) in any man."

Jud. 8. 3, " Then their *anger* (רוּחַ) was abated toward him."

1 Sam. 1. 15, "I am a woman of a *sorrowful spirit* (קְשַׁת רוּחַ, *sorrowful of spirit*)."

1 Kings, 21. 5, " But Jezebel his wife came to him and said unto him, Why is *thy spirit* (רוּחַ) so sad ?"

2 Kings, 2. 15, " The *spirit* (רוּחַ) of Elijah doth rest on Elisha."

1 Chron. 5. 26, " And the God of Israel stirred up the *spirit* (רוּחַ) of Tilgath-pilneser." So also " stirred up the *spirit* (רוּחַ) of the Philistines," 2 Chron. 21, 16. So also of Cyrus, 2 Chron. 30. 22. Ez. 1. 1.

Job, 7. 11, " I will speak in the anguish of *my spirit* (רוּחִי) "

Job, 15. 13, "That thou turnest thy *spirit* (רוּחֲךָ) against God."
" 20. 4, "The *spirit* (רוּחַ) of my understanding causeth me to answer." "Meaning,' says Mr. Barnes, "the emotion of his mind."
" 21. 2, "Why should not *my spirit* (רוּחִי) be troubled ?"
" 32. 8, "But there is a *spirit* (רוּחַ) in man, and the inspiration of the Almighty giveth him understanding"
" 32. 18, "The *spirit* (רוּחַ) within me constraineth me."
Ps. 32, 2, "In whose *spirit* (רוּחַ) there is no guile."
" 34. 18, "And saveth such as be of a contrite *spirit* (רוּחַ)"
" 51. 10, "Renew a right *spirit* (רוּחַ) within me."
" 51. 17, "The sacrifices of God are a broken *spirit* (רוּחַ)."
" 77. 3, "*My spirit* (רוּחִי) was overwhelmed." So also Ps. 142. 3.
" 77. 6, "*My spirit* (רוּחִי) made diligent search."
" 78. 8, "A generation that set not their heart aright, and whose *spirit* (רוּחַ) was not steadfast with God "
Prov. 11. 13, "He that is of a faithful *spirit* (רוּחַ) concealeth the matter."
" 14. 29, "He that is hasty of *spirit* (רוּחַ) exalteth folly."
" 15. 4, "Perverseness therein is a breach in the *spirit* (רוּחַ)."
" 15. 13, "By the sorrow of the heart the *spirit* (רוּחַ) is broken"
" 16. 2, "The Lord weigheth the *spirits* (רוּחוֹת) "
" 16. 18, "Pride goeth before destruction, and an haughty *spirit* (רוּחַ) before a fall."
" 16. 19, "Better is it to be of an humble *spirit* (רוּחַ) than to divide the spoil with the proud."
" 16. 32, "He that ruleth *his spirit* (רוּחוֹ) (is better) than he that taketh a city." So ch. 25. 28.

Prov. 17. 22, "A broken *spirit* (רוּחַ) drieth the bones"
" 17. 27, "A man of understanding is of an excellent *spirit* (רוּחַ)."
" 18. 14, "The *spirit* (רוּחַ) of a man will sustain his infirmity, but a wounded *spirit* (רוּחַ) who can bear?"
" 29. 12, "A fool uttereth all his *mind* (רוּחַ, *spirit*)" That is, a fool gives way to all his impulses
" 29. 23, "Honor shall uphold the humble in *spirit* (רוּחַ)."
Eccl. 1. 14, "All is vanity and vexation of *spirit* (רוּחַ)" So frequently in the context.
" 3 19–21, "For that which befalleth the sons of men befalleth beasts; even one thing befalleth them: as one dieth, so dieth the other; yea, they have all one breath, so that a man hath no preeminence above a beast; for all his vanity All go unto one place, all are of the dust, and all turn to dust again Who knoweth the *spirit* (רוּחַ) of man that goeth upward, and the *spirit* (רוּחַ) of the beast that goeth downward to the earth"

This is usually interpreted of the *vital spirit* of man and beasts, of which the one goes at death upwards, or "returns to God who gave it," while the other goes downwards to the earth, i. e perishes. But we deem it well worthy of question whether the import be not simply, that there is, to the eye of sense, no difference between the destiny of man, whose spirit here on earth *goes* or *aspires* upwards, and that of the beast, whose spirit, or ruling instinct, *tends* or *grovels* downwards to the earth as its appropriate goal In view of the fact that they both die and are turned to dust alike, who can discriminate between the final allotment of a being whose nature *soars to heaven*, and one whose nature *gravitates to earth?* We do not confidently affirm this to be the true sense, but we think it one entitled to attention. As there is no other instance in which רוּחַ is predicated of a beast, it seems reasonable to conclude that it is here used in a tropical sense to indicate the *indoles*, or *genius*, of the beast in opposition to that of man. It is said, indeed, v. 19, that all have one *breath* (רוּחַ), but in this case the allusion is undoubtedly to the *breath of the nostrils*, whereas in v. 21 the term points rather, if we mistake not, to the inner predominant characteristic of a rational nature. However this may be, we are by no means satisfied that the passage, or a fair construction, is designed to teach that brute beasts are possessed of that principle which in man is indicated by the word רוּחַ, *spirit*. But as the beasts evince what may be called a *prevailing bent*, the term may be metaphorically applied to them in this sense. In like manner though the term *heart* is not usually applied as a designation of any part of the nature of a beast, yet in Dan. 4. 16 we find it employed in that reference, but evidently in a metaphorical sense, " Let his *heart* be changed from man's, and let a *beast's heart* be given him." A *beast's spirit* is to be understood in the same way.

Eccl. 7. 8, 9, " The patient in *spirit* (רוּחַ) . . . the proud in *spirit* (רוּחַ) . . . the hasty in *spirit* (רוּחַ)."

" 10. 4, " If the *spirit* (רוּחַ) of the ruler rise up against thee."

Is 4. 4, " When the Lord . . . shall have purged the blood of Jerusalem from the midst thereof by the *spirit* (רוּחַ) of judgment, and by the *spirit* (רוּחַ) of burning."

" 19. 3, " And the *spirit* (רוּחַ) of Egypt shall fail in the midst thereof."

" 19. 14, " The Lord hath mingled a perverse *spirit* (רוּחַ) in the midst thereof."

" 26. 9, " With *my spirit* (רוּחִי) within me will I seek thee early."

" 28. 6, " And for a *spirit* (רוּחַ) of judgment to him that sitteth in judgment."

" 29. 10, " For the Lord hath poured out upon you the *spirit* (רוּחַ) of deep sleep."

" 29. 24. " They also that erred in *spirit* (רוּחַ) shall come to understanding."

Is. 42. 5, "He that giveth breath unto the people upon it, and *spirit* (רוּחַ) to them that walk therein."
" 54. 6, "A woman forsaken and grieved in *spirit* (רוּחַ)"
" 57. 15, "I dwell with him that is of a contrite and humble *spirit* (רוּחַ), to revive the *spirit* (רוּחַ) of the humble." So also ch. 66. 2.
" 57. 16, "For the *spirit* (רוּחַ) should fail before me, and the souls which I have made."
" 61. 3, "The garment of praise for the *spirit* (רוּחַ) of heaviness."
" 65. 14, "But ye shall howl for vexation of *spirit* (רוּחַ)."
Jer. 51. 11, "The Lord hath raised up the *spirit* (רוּחַ) of the kings of the Medes."
Ezek. 1. 12, "Whither the *spirit* (רוּחַ) was to go, they went." That is, whithersoever the *prompting* was to go; and so frequently in the same chapter, and in chap. 10.
" 3. 14, "I went in the heat of *my spirit* (רוּחִי)."
" 11. 5, "For I know the things that come into your *mind* (רוּחַ, *spirit*)"
" 11. 19, "And I will put a new *spirit* (רוּחַ) within you." So also ch. 36. 27.
" 13. 3, "Wo unto the foolish prophets that follow *their own spirit* (רוּחָם)"
" 18. 31, "Make you a new heart and a new *spirit* (רוּחַ)."
" 20. 32, "And that which cometh into *your mind* (רוּחֲכֶם, *your spirits*) shall not be at all."
" 21. 7, "And every heart shall melt . . . and every *spirit* (רוּחַ) shall faint."
Dan. 2. 1, "Nebuchadnezzar dreamed dreams wherewith *his spirit* (רוּחוֹ) was troubled." So v. 3.
Hos. 4. 12, "The *spirit* (רוּחַ) of whoredoms hath caused them to err."
" 9. 7, "The prophet is a fool, and the *spiritual man* (איש רוּחַ, *man of the spirit*) is mad."

Hab. 1. 11, "Then shall *his mind* (רוחו) change, and he shall pass over, and offend."

Zech. 12. 1, "Which layeth the foundation of the earth, and formeth the *spirit* (רוּחַ) of man within him."

" 12. 10, "And I will pour upon the house of David . . . the *spirit* (רוּחַ) of grace and supplications "

Mal. 2 16, "Take heed to *your spirit* (רוּחֲכֶם)."

Mat. 5 3, "Blessed are the poor in *spirit* ($\pi\nu\varepsilon\acute{u}\mu\alpha\tau\iota$)."

Mark, 2. 8, "When Jesus perceived in his *spirit* ($\pi\nu\varepsilon\acute{u}\mu\alpha\tau\iota$)."

" 8. 12, "And he sighed deeply in his *spirit* ($\pi\nu\varepsilon\acute{u}\mu\alpha\tau\iota$)."

Luke, 1. 17, "He shall go before him in the *spirit* ($\pi\nu\varepsilon\acute{u}\mu\alpha\tau\iota$) and power of Elias."

" My *spirit* ($\pi\nu\varepsilon\tilde{\iota}\mu\alpha$) hath rejoiced in God my Saviour."

" 9. 55, "Ye know not what manner of *spirit* ($\pi\nu\varepsilon\acute{u}\mu\alpha\tau o\varsigma$) ye are of."

" 10. 21, "In that hour Jesus rejoiced in *spirit* ($\pi\nu\varepsilon\acute{u}\mu\alpha\tau\iota$).''

1 Cor. 2. 11, "For what man knoweth the things of a man, save the *spirit* ($\pi\nu\varepsilon\tilde{\iota}\mu\alpha$) of man which is in him."

In the following instances we note a marked distinction between *flesh* and *spirit*, which is doubtless equivalent to the distinction that obtains between a *sanctified* and *unsanctified* nature.

Mat 26. 41, "The *spirit* ($\pi\nu\varepsilon\tilde{\iota}\mu\alpha$) indeed is willing, but the flesh is weak."

Rom. 8. 1, "Who walk not after the flesh, but after the *spirit* ($\pi\nu\varepsilon\tilde{\iota}\mu\alpha$) "

" 8. 5, "For they that are after the flesh do mind the things of the flesh; but they that are after the *spirit* ($\pi\nu\varepsilon\tilde{\iota}\mu\alpha$) the things of the *spirit* ($\pi\nu\varepsilon\tilde{\iota}\mu\alpha$).'

" 8. 13, "For if ye live after the flesh ye shall die; but if ye through the *spirit* ($\pi\nu\varepsilon\tilde{\iota}\mu\alpha$) do mortify the deeds of the body, ye shall live."

2 Cor. 7. 1, "Let us cleanse ourselves from all filthiness of the flesh and *spirit* ($\pi\nu\varepsilon\acute{u}\mu\alpha\tau o\varsigma$)."

Gal. 3. 3, " Having begun in the *Spirit* (πνεύματι) are ye now made perfect by the *flesh* ?"
" 5. 17, " For the flesh lusteth against the *Spirit* (πνεῦμα), and the *Spirit* (πνεῦμα) against the flesh."
" 6. 8, " He that soweth to the flesh shall of the flesh reap corruption ; but he that soweth to the *Spirit* (πνεύματι) shall of the *Spirit* (πνεῦμα) reap life everlasting."

(2.) *Spoken of God.*

As the usage under this head is quite extensive, and generally of uniform import, it will be unnecessary to go largely into a detail of passages. It will be observed that in some cases it implies, by anthropopathy, simply the *breath*, according to No. 1, above; in others it points to the divine intelligence; and in still another class to the divine influence or operation,—to that afflatus, impulse, inspiration, or efficacious energy which wrought upon the minds of prophets and holy men of old, whether in inditing the Scriptures or acting as the executors of the divine will in circumstances which required the exercise of supernatural endowments. This species of influence is expressively characterized by the apostle Peter (2 Pet. 1. 21), when he says, " Prophecy came not in old time by the will of man, but holy men of God spake as they were *moved* (φερόμενοι) by the Holy Ghost," where the original term is one that conveys a much stronger idea than that of the gentle sort of impression to which we apply the term " moved." It properly denotes their being *acted by the divine impulse, borne away, rapt, transported*, taken, as it were, out of themselves and possessed entirely by the power of God.

Gen. 1. 2, " The *Spirit* (רוּחַ) of God moved upon the face of the deep." The divine energy.
" 6. 3, " *My Spirit* (רוּחִי) shall not always strive with man."
" 41. 38, " Can we find such an one as this is, a man in whom the *Spirit* (רוּחַ) of God is ?"

Ex. 31. 3, "I have filled him with the *Spirit* (רוּחַ) of God." So ch. 35. 31.

Num. 11. 29, "Would God that all the Lord's people were prophets, and that the Lord would put his *Spirit* (רוּחַ) upon them."

" 24. 2, "And the *Spirit* (רוּחַ) of God came upon him."

2 Sam. 23. 2, "The *Spirit* (רוּחַ) of the Lord spake by me."

1 Kings, 18. 12, "And it shall come to pass, as soon as I am gone from thee, that the *Spirit* (רוּחַ) of the Lord shall carry thee whither I know not."

Thou shalt be *rapt* in the Spirit in such a manner that thy body shall be transported away. Thus Acts, 8. 39, "And when they were come up out of the water, the Spirit of the Lord *caught away* Philip, that the eunuch saw him no more."

1 Chron. 28. 12, "And the pattern of all that he had by the *Spirit* (רוּחַ)."

Job, 26. 13, "By his *Spirit* (רוּחַ) he hath garnished the heavens." By his omnipotent *operation*. "There is no evidence," says Mr. Barnes, "that Job refers to the Third Person of the Trinity, the Holy Spirit, as being specially engaged in the work of creation."

Job, 33. 4, "The *Spirit* (רוּחַ) of God hath made me, and the breath of the Almighty hath given me life." Sense the same as in the preceding.

Ps. 18. 15, "The foundations of the world were discovered at thy rebuke, O Lord, at the blast of the *breath* (רוּחַ) of thy nostrils."

" 33. 6, "By the word of the Lord were the heavens made, and all the hosts of them by the *breath* (רוּחַ) of his mouth."

" 51. 11, 12, "Take not thy Holy *Spirit* (רוּחַ) from me . . . and uphold me with thy free *Spirit* (רוּחַ)."

Ps 104. 30, "Thou sendest forth *thy Spirit* (רוּחֲךָ), they are created."

" 139. 7, "Whither shall I go from *thy Spirit* (רוּחֲךָ)?"

Zech. 4. 6, "Not by might, nor by power, but by *my Spirit* (רוּחִי), saith the Lord."

In a single instance we find the phrase " spirit of God" used to denote the human spirit or life as the product of the divine.

Job, 27. 3, "All the while my breath is in me, and the *spirit* (רוּחַ) of God is in my nostrils"

Mat. 4. 1, "Then was Jesus led up of the *Spirit* (πνεύματι) into the wilderness." So also Mark, 1. 12.

" 10. 20, "For it is not ye that speak, but the *Spirit* (πνεῦμα) of your Father which speaketh in you."

" 12. 18, "I will put my *Spirit* (πνεῦμα) upon him, and he shall show judgment to the Gentiles."

Luke, 1. 80, "The child grew, and waxed strong in *spirit* (πνεύματι)."

" 4 14, "Then Jesus returned in the power of the *Spirit* (πνεύματος) into Galilee"

John, 3 34, "God giveth not the *Spirit* (πνεῦμα) by measure unto him."

" 4. 24, "God is a *Spirit* (πνεῦμα), and they that worship him must worship him in *spirit* (πνεύματι) and in truth."

This might be rendered without the article, which is wanting in the original, "God is spirit," as the design seems to be to indicate the *moral* character of the Deity, rather than any *metaphysical* attribute of his being. God is essentially of the same nature with the influences of his Spirit, and therefore he is to be correspondently worshipped.

John, 6. 63, "It is the *Spirit* (πνεῦμα) that quickeneth; the words that I speak unto you, they are *spirit* (πνεῦμα) and they are life."

Acts, 2. 4, "They spake as the *Spirit* (πνεῦμα) gave them utterance."

Acts, 6 10, "And they were not able to resist the wisdom and the *spirit* (πνεύματι) by which he spake."

" 8. 29, "Then the *Spirit* (πνεῦμα) said unto Philip, Go near and join thyself to this chariot."

§ 6.

רוּחַ *in the sense of a Spirit, a Personal Agent, whether good or bad, whether spoken of Angels, Demons, or Men.*

1 Sam. 16. 14, "But the Spirit of the Lord departed from Saul, and an evil *spirit* (רוּחַ) from the Lord troubled him." So also v. 15, 16, 23, ch. 18. 10; 19. 9

Had we no evidence from other sources of the existence and agency of such spirits, we might here and elsewhere understand by the term *evil disposition, perverse prompting* which is said to be from the Lord, because the result of that providential discipline which he exercises over all men, good and bad, and which, as in the case of the hardening of Pharaoh's heart, is said to effect what it merely permits and overrules. But as the Scriptures clearly acquaint us with the fact of the being and influence of such spirits, both angelic and demoniacal, there is nothing to prevent the terms being understood in this and all similar places of real personal entities of a supernatural order.

1 Kings, 22 21, 22, "And there came forth a *spirit* (רוּחַ) and stood before the Lord, and said, I will persuade him. And the Lord said unto him, Wherewith? And he said, I will go forth, and I will be a lying *spirit* (רוּחַ) in the mouth of all his prophets." So also v. 23

Job, 4. 15, "Then a *spirit* (רוּחַ) stood before my face."

Zech 13. 2, "And I will cause the prophets and the unclean *spirit* (רוּחַ) to pass out of the land."

Mat. 10. 1, "He gave them power against unclean *spirits* (πνεύματα)." And thus in a multitude of instances of "casting out *unclean spirits*."

Luke, 10. 20, "In this rejoice not that the *spirits* (πνεύματα) are subject unto you."

" 24. 39, "For a *spirit* (πνεῦμα) hath not flesh and bones as ye see me have."

By this is doubtless meant a phantom, such as Job describes, and of which he says, "I could not discern the form thereof; an image was before mine eyes," i. e. a shadowy resemblance of a human form. See my work on the "Resurrection of Christ."

Heb. 1. 14, "Are they not all ministering *spirits* (πνεύματα), sent forth to minister for them who shall be heirs of salvation?"

Acts, 23. 8, "For the Sadducees say that there is no resurrection, neither angel, nor *spirit* (πνεῦμα)."

" 23. 9, "But if an angel or *spirit* (πνεῦμα) hath spoken to him, let us not fight against God."

Heb. 12. 22, 23, "Ye are come . . . to the *spirits* (πνεύματα) of just men made perfect."

1 Pet. 3. 19, "By which also he went and preached unto the *spirits* (πνεύμασι) in prison."

The induction of examples presented above can scarcely fail to authorize the conclusion already suggested, that the word *spirit*, in reference to man, denotes a higher element of his nature than the word usually rendered *soul*. It is indeed unquestionable that in a multitude of cases it is impossible to distinguish between them, or to assign a reason why the one should, in a particular connexion, be employed rather than the other. In such passages, for example, as the following, it seems impossible to discover why ψυχή in the first might not be, with the utmost propriety, substituted for πνεῦμα in the second, and so *vice versa:* Gen. 35. 18, "And it came to pass as her *soul* (נֶפֶשׁ, ψυχή) was in departing." Eccl. 12. 7, "And the *spirit* (רוּחַ, πνεῦμα) shall return to God who gave it." So Ps 88. 4, "My *soul* (נַפְשִׁי) is full of troubles." Job, 21. 4, "Why should not *my spirit* (רוּחִי) be troubled?" Thus too Ps. 119. 28, "*My soul* (נַפְשִׁי) melteth for heaviness." Ps. 77. 4, "*My spirit* (רוּחִי) is overwhelmed." What assignable difference can be suggested in the import of the two words in these connexions?

The case is rendered still more striking where the same Hebrew term (רוּחַ) is rendered variously in the Greek, as Gen. 41. 8, "And it came to pass in the morning that his *spirit* (רוּחַ, ψυχή) was troubled." Is. 19. 3, "And the *spirit* (רוּחַ, πνεῦμα) of Egypt shall be troubled." A similar diversity of usage obtains in the Greek of the New Testament. John, 12. 27, "Now is my *soul* (ψυχή) troubled." John, 13. 21, "When Judas had thus said he was troubled *in spirit* (τῷ πνεύματι)." How, moreover, it may be asked, is "anguish of *soul* (נֶפֶשׁ, ψυχή)," Gen. 41. 21, to be distinguished from "anguish of *spirit* (רוּחַ, πνεῦμα)," Ex. 6. 9; or " bitterness of *soul*," Job, 21. 25, from ' bitterness of *spirit*," Gen. 26. 35? The identity of import in these texts is obvious, and the list might be greatly increased, and yet it is equally clear that in a vast multitude of instances a marked distinction is kept up, and forms of phraseology occur where the substitution of one for the other would violate the fixed analogy of diction, whether we can settle the grounds of that diction or not. Thus we never meet with the expressions "smiting the *spirit*"—"persecuting the *spirit*"—"lurking privily for the *spirit*," nor of the *spirit's* "hungering," "thirsting," "famishing," "being emptied," "filled," "satisfied," "living," "dying," "being destroyed," "being consumed," &c.—all these being affections predicable rather of the *soul* as a principle more nearly allied to the physical or corporeal, than we usually conceive of the higher and more spiritual element in our constitution. So on the other hand we meet with certain appropriated uses of the term *spirit* which would not admit, according to analogy, of the substitution of *soul;* as for example when the *spirit* is said to be "given," "put," or "poured" upon any one, to "rest" upon one, to "come upon" one, to "go up" from one, to "come forth" from one, to be "turned against" one, to be "ruled," to be "renewed," to "enter into" one, &c. This language is never used of the *soul* So also no instances occur of the use of *soul* in such phrases as "*spirit* of wisdom," "*spirit* of jealousy," "*spirit* of judgment," "*spirit* of slumber," "*spirit* of meekness," &c.

On the whole we think it will appear that, as a general fact, the *affections* denoted by the word *spirit* are of a superior grade to those denoted by *soul*, and that, of consequence, the *subject* to which they pertain is of a higher nature. The evidence of this will rise upon us in proportion to the evidence that exists, derived from other forms of speech, that there is a real distinction intended to be affirmed between them. But how can we avoid this conviction with such language before us as the following? 1 Thes 5. 23, "And I pray God your whole *spirit*, and *soul*, and *body*, be preserved blameless unto the coming of our Lord Jesus Christ." We are aware that this is often understood as merely recognizing, without sanctioning, a distinction that was popularly embraced in ancient times, and that the apostle's design was simply to intimate by a cumulative form of expression that he desired the preservation blameless of the *whole man* with all his powers, faculties, and affections, while at the same time he had no purpose of pointing to a threefold metaphysical division of the elements of human nature. But it must be admitted as in the highest degree probable, that if there actually *is* such a distinction it is alluded to in these words of the apostle. But that such a tripartite distinction in man is inevitably to be conceded is clear from the fact that he possesses some principle in addition to the $\psi\nu\chi\dot{\eta}$ which distinguishes him from the beasts of the field. This can be no other than the $\pi\nu\varepsilon\ddot{\nu}\mu\alpha$ or *spirit*, between which and the *body* the $\psi\nu\chi\dot{\eta}$ or *soul* is an intermediate element.

This distinction was clearly recognized in the ancient philosophies. The τρίμερὴς ὑπόστασις σώματος, πνεύματος, καὶ ψυχῆς, the *three-parted hypostasis of body, spirit, and soul* was familiar even among the fathers of the Christian Church, of whom no one is more explicit than Irenæus.* "There are three things of which the entire perfect man consists—flesh, soul, spirit—the one, the spirit, giving form, the other, the flesh, receiving form. The soul is intermediate between these two, and sometimes following the spirit is elevated by it, and sometimes consenting to the flesh falls into earthly concupiscences."

Origen speaks with equal distinctness to the same effect.† "There is a threefold partition of man, the Body, or flesh, the lowest part of our nature, on which the old serpent by original sin inscribed the law of sin, and by which we are tempted to vile things, and as oft as we are overcome by the temptation are joined fast to the devil; the Spirit, by which we express the likeness of the divine nature, in which the Creator, from the archetype of his own mind, engraved the eternal law of the honest by his own

---

* "Tria sunt ex quibus perfectus homo constat, carne, anima, spiritu, altero quidem figurante, spiritu, altero quod formatur, carne. Id vero, quod inter hæc est duo, est anima, quæ aliquando subsequens spiritum elevatur ab eo, aliquando autem consentiens carni decidit in terrenas concupiscentias." *Lib* v c. 1.

† Triplex hominis portio, corpus, seu caro, infirma nostri pars, cui per genitatem culpam legem inscripsit peccati serpens ille veterator, quâque ad turpia provocamur, ac victi, diabolo nectimur; spiritus, quo divinæ naturæ similitudinem exprimimus, in qua Conditor Optimus de suæ mentis archetypo, eternam istam honesti legem insculpsit digito, h. e. spiritu suo, hoc Deo conglutinamur, unumque cum Deo, reddimur; Porro tertia, et inter ea media, anima, quæ velut in factiosa republica non potest non alterutri partium accedere, hinc atque hinc solicitatur, liberum habet utro velit inclinari; si carni renuncians ad spiritûs partes sese nduxerit fiet et ipsa spiritualis, sin ad carnis cupiditates abjecerit, degenerabit et ipsa in corpus. *Sup. Epist ad Rom* L. 1

finger, and by which we are firmly conjoined to Him and made one with Him; and then the Soul, intermediate between these two, and which, as in a factious commonwealth, cannot but join with one or other of the former parties, being solicited this way and that, and having liberty to which it will adhere. If it renounce the flesh and join with the spirit, it will itself become spiritual; but if it cast itself down to the desires of the flesh, it will itself degenerate into the body."

It would be easy to multiply indefinitely quotations to this effect from similar sources, clearly setting forth a distinction which is clearly recognized in holy writ. Thus the apostle says, Heb. 4 12, "For the word of God is quick and powerful, sharper than any two-edged sword, piercing even to the dividing asunder of *soul* and *spirit*" That is, it penetrates with such a searching and discriminating power into the secret recesses of man's nature as to separate, like the knife of the dissector, things that are most closely joined together, and even to make a severance, as it were, between elements so intimately related to each other as the soul and spirit.*

---

* Mr Barnes (in loc) thus comments upon this passage "The former word here, $\psi v \chi \eta$, *soul*, is evidently used to denote the *animal life*, as distinguished from the mind or soul The latter word, $\pi v \epsilon \tilde{v} \mu a$, *spirit*, means the soul, the immaterial and immortal part, that which lives when the animal life is extinct. This distinction occurs in 1 Thes 5 23, 'Your whole spirit, and soul, and body,' and it is a distinction which we are constantly in the habit of making. There is the body in man— the animal life—and the immortal part that leaves the body when life is extinct Mysteriously united, they constitute one man. When the animal life is separated from the soul, or when the soul leaves the animated body, the body dies, and life is extinct " This language is correct as far as it recognizes the distinction between the two principles of soul and spirit, but it is marked by some confusion in the use of terms, and by what we must deem an erroneous view of the true psychology of our nature, for (1) It gives the designation *soul* to the *spirit* instead of the *animal life*, which is directly contrary to the obvious purpose of the apostle The

In the Alexandrian philosophy in particular, which favored the Pythagorean and Platonic, the distinction above

ψυχὴ is the *animal life* or *soul* in express contradistinction from the πνεῦμα or *spirit*, being the principle which man possesses in common with the lower animals. To take the term *soul* from this application and bestow it upon the *spirit* is entirely unwarranted. In strict propriety the *soul* denotes the *psychical* principle, and that only. (2.) Equally unwarranted is the intimation conveyed in the sentence in which it is asserted, that 'the πνεῦμα, *spirit*, denotes the immaterial and immortal part, that which lives *when the animal life is extinct.*' In strictness of speech the *animal life* in man, in the sense in which Mr Barnes here uses the phrase, is *never* extinct, because that life is denoted by ψυχὴ, and the human ψυχὴ never dies. What the ψυχὴ is to the life *in* the body that it is to it *out of* the body, not indeed from the immortality of its own nature, for in that case the beasts would be immortal, but from its connexion with the πνεῦμα, which is the true ground of man's immortal life, as it is by this that he is conjoined to the Deity, the great and only fountain of life. Life is not an object of creation. It is a perpetual influx from God. The receptacle of animal life, which in man is the ψυχὴ, is created, and is just as much the subject of influent life after death as before. "When the soul leaves the animated body, the body dies, and life is extinct." The life of the body is extinct, but not the life of that which animated the body, i. e. the ψυχὴ. The life of the caterpillar-body is extinct when the butterfly is evolved, because that life has now passed into the butterfly-body; the butterfly-body, however, remains still a mere receptacle of life. So with the life of man. His soul (ψυχὴ) is not life, but a receptacle of life. The life of beasts, which is also but influx, returns and is reabsorbed into the infinite ocean of life, and the psychical vehicle is resolved back into its primitive elements.

The relation of the ψυχὴ to the vital processes of the animal body is undoubtedly a subject involved in great obscurity, and one that forms the grand problem of physiology. Hitherto all efforts have been abortive to establish the existence of what is termed a *vital principle* as a physical agency in the elaboration and nutrition of the various organisms of the body. These organisms and their functions are beyond question the effects of a cause—the result of some kind of organific potency which we denominate *life*. It is we think equally unquestionable, that this last principle operates *through* the ψυχὴ as an intermediate agent, inasmuch as when the ψυχὴ leaves the body these processes all cease, and *life* is most adequately studied from the phenomena of its opposite, *death*. Still we are not competent to affirm that the ψυχὴ is itself *identical* with

mentioned is very plainly recognized, as they denominated the πνεῦμα as the *rational soul* (νοῦς, τὸ λογικὸν, *mind, that which reasons*), and the ψυχὴ, the *sensitive soul* (τὸ ἐπιθυμητικόν, *that which desires or lusts*). Josephus also gives us intimations to the same effect. Thus, in his account of the creation (J. A. Lib. I. c. 1. § 2), he says, "God took dust from the ground, and formed man, and inserted in him *a spirit and a soul* (πνεῦμα καὶ ψυχήν). Thus too in the apocryphal book of Wisdom, ch. 15. 11, "Forasmuch as he knew not his Maker, and him that inspired into him the *soul* (ψυχὴν) that worketh, and that breathed into him a living *spirit* (πνεῦμα)." In the book of Enoch, likewise apocryphal, (apud Fabric. Cod. Pseudep. p. 190,) we find mention made of τὰ πνεύματα τῶν ψυχῶν τῶν ἀποθανόντων ἀνθρώπων, *the spirits of the souls of deceased men;* and

---

the vital power, any more than we can say that the brain is a thinking substance, because it is by means of it that thought is carried on in the present life. To our perception throughout a great part of the physical universe what may be termed the *instrumental* cause acts as one with the *principal*, which is in all cases the divine energy operating by influx. In the animal world, including man with all the other tribes, the ψυχὴ is most undoubtedly the element to which we are proximately to refer the vital processes, but still as a created medium or receptacle of the primary influent power of life, which is not created, but perpetually *flows* from the infinite source of all life. When therefore we predicate a vitalizing power of the ψυχὴ, and consider it as the organific agent which originally forms the body, and continually repairs its waste, we are not to lose sight of the fact that the real agency is the divine uncreated life acting in conjunction with the created mediate principle called the ψυχὴ. But this may be familiarly illustrated. In contemplating a steamboat in motion we distinguish three leading parts—the steam, the machinery, and the body or framework of the boat. The steam, the motive power, is the *life* or *spirit* of the whole, but this power acts immediately on the machinery. Now suppose the machinery thus acted upon by the steam, to be endowed with the power of forming or elaborating the body of the boat. This supposition will perhaps give us as clear an idea as we can form of the office of the ψυχὴ in its vital relations to the body. But we must be content with the simple fact. The *mode* of the operation inevitably eludes our ken.

again (p. 196), *τὰ πνεύματα τὰ ἐνπορευόμενα ἀπὸ τῆς ψυχῆς αὐτῶν, ὡς ἐκ τῆς σαρκὸς*, *spirits going forth from their soul as from the flesh*. For ourselves we read in these extracts the intimations of a great psychological fact, viz., that the *πνεῦμα* is to the *ψυχή*—the *spirit* to the *soul*—what the soul is to the body. The *soul* (*ψυχή*) is a kind of involucrum to the *spirit* (*πνεῦμα*), which Plato calls the *εἴδωλον*, *image*, of the spirit. This *ψυχή* is the *spiritual body* or the *body of the spirit*, so called, however, not as denoting its true ontological nature, which is *psychical*, but rather its *uses*, as constituting the *form* through which the *affections of the spirit* manifest themselves.*

We are well aware of the difficulties which crowd upon our conceptions of this subject, from the fact that the ordinary usage of the word *body* suggests ideas drawn from material substances and forms. But as we have scriptural authority for the use of the phrase "spiritual *body*," we must deem ourselves at full liberty to employ it in this con-

---

* "Visible form, or shape, including the mere internal organization, of which we become aware by research and observation, are but the outer appearances of the true form, because that is, abstractly considered, only the *mode* of being. But the visible external form corresponds to and represents the true internal form. By this it is not meant that there is an inner shape, of which visible shape is the image, but that the order, beauty, and adaptation to use of the true form are represented and revealed by the visible form, because of the correspondence between them. Thus, when more is known of the soul of man, it will be seen that its faculties, proportions, functions, and enjoyments, all exist in their own form, and are all represented by the corresponding visible form, which is its instrument and clothing. When this relation is seen, it will be readily believed, that the soul without a body is naked, joyless, nay impossible ; that it must therefore have a spiritual body in the spiritual world. And this body must be the image of the material body, because the material body, being already in perfect correspondence with the soul, and so its perfectly adapted envelope, a spiritual body not in its image would be less perfectly adapted to be for ever its dwelling and instrument." *Parsons' Essays*, p. 111. Boston, 1845.

nexion, notwithstanding any possible conflict with previous ideas. It is undoubtedly true that the term *body* is for the most part applied in common language to sensible material substances, yet as no word could be found *more* adapted to convey the idea intended, we see no reason for forbearing its use. It is inevitable, from the nature of the case, that spiritual objects should be denoted by terms drawn from the material world, and the mind naturally modifies their import according to the innate exigencies of the subject. In the present instance we regard it as *certain* that there is, in the constitution of man, a principle properly denominated ψυχή, which is the true seat and subject of what is usually called *bodily sensation.* It is *certain*, too, that this principle lives after death, and lives in connexion with another element of our nature called πνεῦμα, by which man is distinguished from the beasts that perish. These substances are both beyond the reach of our senses, and the intrinsic qualities of each baffle our comprehension; yet from the relation which we are forced to conceive of their sustaining to each other, we scruple not to say that the one is the *body* to the other. As it is through the gross material body that the ψυχή manifests itself in the present world, so we are warranted to infer that it is through the ψυχή that the πνεῦμα manifests itself in the other world; in other words, it performs for the πνεῦμα the office of a *body*, and is consequently so termed. As to the question of *material* and *immaterial*, we do not concede the justice of the demand, that we should attempt discriminations on this head, which our ignorance of the *essence* of matter and of *spirit* renders us incompetent. The point we are considering is one of *scriptural usage* and not of *philosophical verity.* The difficulty, on this score, is no greater and no other on our view than on that of the opposite view, if there be any opposite view. We do not see how it can be denied that the distinction for which we contend does exist. Man is assuredly at once *psychical* and *spiritual.* These epithets irresistibly refer themselves to two distinct principles of our being. The assertion of this fact imposes not upon the one party any more than the other the obligation of defining the intrinsic nature and properties of the two principles. Call the ψυχή what you please, *material* or *immaterial*. We know nothing about *essence* of either; but we know enough of the *relation* of the ψυχή to the πνεῦμα to affirm that it is to it *a body* in the sense in which that term applies itself to subjects of this supersensuous nature.

From the remarks now made the reader can scarcely be left in a mistake as to the true import which we think to be attached to the phrase *spiritual body*. *Spiritual* in this connexion is not to be understood in a metaphysical sense as distinguished from *material*, but in a moral sense as distinguished from *fleshly, fallen, sensual*. Metaphysically speaking the appropriate term is *psychical body*, but as the term *psychical*, like the term *fleshly*, has two senses, the one alluding to, but not defining, the *substance* called ψυχή, the other to the *character* superinduced upon it by sin; and as the apostle is here expressly contrasting the σῶμα ψυχικόν, *natural body*, with the σῶμα πνευματικόν, *spiritual body*, in moral rather than metaphysical respects, we must be governed in our interpretation by this fact. No confusion of ideas will result if we simply bear in mind, that as a *fleshly body* pertains both to saint and sinner, but in the one case as denoting *sinful, sensual, corrupt*, and in the other that which is *composed of flesh*, so also the term *psychical* is used with equal latitude. The *spiritual* man does not, by regeneration, cease to be *psychical* in the sense of having a ψυχή, but simply in the sense of having the ψυχή predominant in its *sensual influences* over the πνεῦμα in its *spiritual* or *holy* influences. It is only in its latter import that the apostle uses the term when speaking of the σῶμα ψυχικόν, *the psychical body*. Let this distinction be once understood, and the train of his reasoning will be disembarrassed of all difficulty as to any apparent conflict with the views of psychology developed in the preceding pages *

A difficulty may here however be suggested, founded upon what we have elsewhere affirmed to be a fact of Revelation, that the wicked are not represented as partaking, in a true and genuine sense, of *the* Resurrection. Our Lord does indeed assert that "they that have done evil (shall come forth) unto the resurrection of damnation." But it is undeniable that the general tone of the New Testament declarations is quite different from this, and that too from the very necessity of the case. We have several times adverted to the fact of the intimate and indissoluble connexion between the *regeneration* and the *resurrection* of the saints. Their *eternal life* ($ζωή$), in the resurrection-state, is the completed issue of their *spiritual life* commenced here on earth in the quickening of their souls by the Holy Ghost from the death of trespasses and sins. This change is certainly not wrought upon wicked men, living and dying such, and how can they be subjects of the *effect* when they are not the subjects of the *cause*?

The conclusion is inevitable if the inspired representations on this theme be admitted. As the saints die to sin

---

* As I have inadvertently remarked in the work on the "Resurrection" (p 115) that $ψυχικός$ is *always* in the New Testament rendered *natural*, I will here adduce all the instances, besides those in 1 Cor 15, where the word occurs 1 Cor 2 14, "But the *natural man* ($ψυχικὸς ἄνθρωπος$) receiveth not the things of the Spirit of God, for they are foolishness to him, neither can he know them, because they are spiritually discerned' James, 3. 15, "This wisdom descendeth not from above, but is earthly, *sensual* ($ψυχικη$), and devilish" Jude, 19, "These be they who separate themselves, *sensual* ($ψυχικοί$), not having the Spirit." The whole number of cases is six, in four of which it is rendered *natural*, and in two *sensual* In all of them its import is *moral* and not *metaphysical* As however the term $ψυχη$ denotes what we may term a *metaphysical* element in our nature, the fact of general usage offers no bar in the way of the sense which we assign to the epithet in reference to that part of man's constitution which survives death

by reason of their mystic relation to the death of Christ, so they rise to newness of life on the ground of their relation to the virtue of his resurrection. "For if we be planted together in the likeness of his death, we shall be also in the likeness of his resurrection . . . Now if we be dead with Christ, we believe that we shall also live with him; knowing that Christ being raised from the dead dieth no more; death hath no more dominion over him. For in that he died, he died unto sin once; but in that he liveth, he liveth unto God. Likewise reckon ye yourselves to be dead indeed unto sin, but alive unto God through Jesus Christ our Lord." Here is the germ of the resurrection-life. So again, "Buried with him in baptism, wherein also ye are risen with him through the faith of the operation of God, who hath raised him from the dead. And you being dead in your sins, and the uncircumcision of your flesh, hath he quickened together with him." Once more, "If then ye be risen with Christ, seek those things which are above, where Christ sitteth on the right hand of God." Nothing can be more obvious, from the tenor of these passages, than the indissoluble bond of union which connects the spiritual life of his people with the resurrection-life of Jesus, and it is a life which must necessarily, in the end issue out into a finished resurrection with them also. This is in fact the law of resurrection with all its happy participants. They have begun even here to live their eternal life. The deposition of the mortal body is a mere circumstance in the career of their immortal and beatified existence. As they have already been *raised* in Christ, their future life after being loosed from clay is a resurrection life of course, because it was a resurrection-life *before* that event. Their dismissal from the body leaves their true life just what it was. And if it *was* a resurrection-life it *will be,* equally as a matter of course, in a resurrection-body.

This will be the true resurrection, because it is the true life. But this resurrection cannot pertain to the wicked, because this life does not pertain to them. But do not the wicked *live* hereafter? To this we reply, In the same sense in which they *live* here. Nothing is more certain than that they *exist*, and yet nothing is at the same time more certain than that they do not *live* in the sense which is affirmed of the righteous. How can they truly *live* if they are *dead* in trespasses and sins? The fact is, the distinction in the *life* of the two classes is the distinction of the ζωή and the ψυχή. The wicked in the present world live the life of the ψυχή, and in the other world they live the same. Their bodies there are *psychical bodies,* in the *character* of psychical, i. e. sensual, corrupt, sinful, just as their *fleshly* bodies here are *fleshly* in the same sense. The bodies of the saints there are also *psychical,* but in a different sense, just as their bodies here were *fleshly* in a different sense. They are now become πνεύματικα, *spiritual* bodies, because they are acted by the life of the πνεῦμα, or *spirit,* which cannot be affirmed of the wicked. Now as it is this latter life which is alone denominated *life,* so it is the resurrection alone of these spiritual bodies which is truly called *resurrection,* and of this the wicked cannot partake, for the simple reason that they do not partake of the *life* which it involves. As to the words of our Saviour before alluded to, where he speaks of the doers of evil coming forth to the "resurrection of damnation," we leave it to every one to interpret them as best he may, consistently with the expositions now given, the soundness of which we hold to be beyond the reach of denial, if there is any thing explicitly taught in Revelation. For ourselves we have no difficulty in regarding it as an *accommodated* and *tropical* form of speech. *Resurrection* signifies etymologically *rising again;* and as the wicked enter at death upon a *continued existence,* they may be said in that sense *to rise;* but not in the sense in which *resurrection* is predicated of the righteous. A "resurrection of damnation" is precisely the opposite of a "resurrection of life."

CHAPTER IV.

נְשָׁמָה: *(neshâmàh), πνοή (pnoë), Breath, Spirit.*

This is a term applied occasionally to the *soul* or *spirit* of man, and like the preceding נֶפֶשׁ and רוּחַ, has also primitively the import of *breath* or *breathing*. Its verbal root, נָשַׁם, *to breathe*, is obsolete, but is doubtless to be classed with the family of words having the same sense, viz נָשַׁב, נָשַׁף, and by transposition נֶפֶשׁ. The twofold usage of נְשָׁמָה is exhibited in the following passages, embracing all the instances in which it occurs

§ 1.

נְשָׁמָה *in the sense of Breath*

Gen. 2. 7, "And the Lord God formed man of the dust of the ground, and breathed into him the *breath of life* (נִשְׁמַת חַיִּים)."

" 7 22, "All in whose nostrils was the *breath of life* (נִשְׁמַת־רוּחַ חַיִּים, *the breath of the spirit of life*)."

Deut. 20. 16, "Thou shalt save alive nothing that *breatheth* (כָּל־נְשָׁמָה, *every thing that breatheth* Concr. *for living or breathing thing*)"

Josh. 10 40, "He left none remaining, but utterly destroyed *every thing that breathed* (כָּל־הַנְּשָׁמָה, Concr. *every breathing thing*)"

" 11 11, "There was not any left to *breathe* (כָּל־נְשָׁמָה, Concr. *every breathing thing*)" So also v. 14

2 Sam. 22. 16, "At the rebuking of the Lord, *at the blast of the breath of his nostrils* (מִנִּשְׁמַת רוּחַ אַפּוֹ)." So also Ps 18 15

1 Kings, 15 29, "He left not to Jeroboam *any that breathed* (כָּל־נְשָׁמָה, Conc. *every breathing thing*)."

1 Kings, 17. 17, "And his sickness was so sore, that there was no *breath* (נְשָׁמָה) left in him."

Job, 4. 9, "By the *blast* (נִשְׁמַת) of God they perish."

" 27. 3, "All the while *my breath* (נִשְׁמָתִי) is in me, and the spirit of God is in my nostrils."

" 32. 8, "But there is a spirit in man, and the *inspiration of the Almighty* (נִשְׁמַת שַׁדַּי) giveth them understanding."

" 33. 4, "The Spirit of God hath made me, and the *breath of the Almighty* (נִשְׁמַת שַׁדַּי) hath given me life."

The original expression in this and the preceding verse is precisely the same, and it is fair to infer that the meaning is the same. The LXX render in both cases by πνοή, *breath*, and the remote allusion is undoubtedly to the *inbreathing* of the Almighty into the frame of man when first created, and by which he became a *living soul*.

Job, 34. 14, "If he gather unto himself his spirit and *his breath* (נִשְׁמָתוֹ)."

" 37. 10, "By the *breath* (נִשְׁמַת) of God frost is given."

Ps. 150. 6, "Let every thing that hath *breath* (נְשָׁמָה) praise the Lord."

Is. 2. 22, "Cease ye from man, whose *breath* (נְשָׁמָה) is in his nostrils."

" 30. 33, "The *breath* (נִשְׁמַת) of the Lord, like a stream of brimstone, doth kindle it."

" 42. 5, "He that giveth *breath* (נְשָׁמָה) unto the people upon it."

Dan. 5. 23, "God in whose hand thy *breath* (נִשְׁמְתָא) is."

" 10. 17, "Neither is there *breath* (נְשָׁמָה) left in me."

§ 2.

נְשָׁמָה *in the sense of Mind, the Intelligent Principle.*

Job, 26. 4, "To whom hast thou uttered words? and whose *spirit* (נְשָׁמָה) came from thee?"

That is, says Mr. Barnes (in loc.), "by whose spirit didst thou speak? What claim hast thou to inspiration, or to the uttering of sentiments beyond what man could originate? The meaning is, that there was nothing remarkable in what he had said, that would show that he had been indebted for it either to God, or to the wise and good on earth."

Prov. 20. 27, "The *spirit* (נְשָׁמָה) of man is the candle of the Lord, searching the inward parts of the belly."

'Spirit' seems here to stand as a designation of the intelligence acting in the office of conscience, whose function it is to investigate and examine the inmost recesses of the heart. The words of the apostle, 1 Cor. 2. 11, are strikingly parallel; "What man knoweth the things of a man (his concealed thoughts and designs. Macknight,) save the spirit of a man which is in him?"

Is. 57. 16, "For the spirit should fail before me, and the *souls* (נְשָׁמוֹת) which I have made."

This Gesenius understands as equivalent to *vital breath*, ψυχή, thus according with נֶפֶשׁ, No. 2. It seems, however, more naturally to convey the idea of *reasonable souls*.

The above are all the cases in which נְשָׁמָה occurs, and in only three of them do we recognize the sense of *intelligence* equivalent to *spirit* or *mind*. The use of the term therefore throws no special light upon the main theme of our inquiry. We give the instances, however, to illustrate the various diction of the Scriptures in regard to the general subject.

CHAPTER V.

לֵב *(lēb)*, καρδία *(kardia), Heart.*

THIS word is also in all probability a primitive, though referred by lexicographers to the assumed verbal root לָבַב, of which the supposed meaning is *to be fat*. "The primary idea," says Gesenius, "lies in the *slipperiness*, lubricity, of fat things; which notion is expressed by the syllables לב, לה; see חָלַב *to be fat*, חָלָה, חָלַק, שָׁלַט, *to be smooth, slippery;*

Sansc. *lip, to besmear, to anoint.* Hence לֵב, לֵבָב, (לְבָה),
the heart, as covered with fat, and therefore called also
חֵלֶב, *fat.*" The word, like each of the preceding, yields
also a denominative נִלְבַב, which signifies privatively *to be
without heart,* i. e. *to want understanding.* The relation of
the substantive לֵב to the verb as a radical is so slight that
we may justly consider it as a primitive, and in all probability as the parent source of our English word *live,* whence
life. Rothe, in his "Psychologia Veteris Testamenti," p.
40, observes that in the Hebrew anthropology the blood is
preeminently the seat of life, (see Gen. 9. 4), and as the
heart is the fountain of the blood, it was a natural process
to make the heart the seat and centre of the vital principle.
This may account indeed for the formation of terms in
our own and other languages traceable more or less to the
Hebrew, though it can scarcely be deemed sufficient to establish the truth of the doctrine. It is certain, however, that
the sacred writers make the *heart,* in an eminent sense, the
seat of *sensation, emotion,* and *affection,* and so completely
does this metaphorical sense of the term predominate over
the literal, that comparatively few instances can be adduced
where it bears unequivocally the import of that leading
member of the human viscera. The following passages
disclose the usage which comes nearest to the one in question, and even in regard to several of these it still remains doubtful whether the figurative sense is not the true
one.

§ 1.

לב *in the sense of Heart as a Physical Organ of the Body.*

Ex. 28. 29, " And Aaron shall bear the names of the children of Israel in the breast-plate of judgment upon *his
heart* (לבו)."

2 Sam. 18. 14, " And he took three darts in his hand, and
thrust them through the *heart* (לב) of Absalom while
he was yet alive "

2 Kings, 9 24, "And the arrow went out at *his heart* (לִבּוֹ), and he sunk down in his chariot."

Prov. 4 30, "A sound *heart* (לֵב) is the life of the flesh."

Cant. 8 6, "Set me as a seal upon *thine heart* (לִבֶּךָ)." Doubtful.

Is. 1. 5, "The whole head is sick, and the whole *heart* (לֵבָב) is faint." Probably figurative.

Jer. 4. 19, "I am pained at *my very heart* (קִירוֹת לִבִּי, *the walls of my heart*); my *heart* (לִבִּי) maketh a noise in me."

Ezek. 11. 19, "I will take the stony *heart* (לֵב) out of their flesh, and will give them an *heart* (לֵב) of flesh." So also, 36 26 This, however, may be understood metaphorically.

Hos. 13. 8, "I will meet them as a bear that is bereaved of her whelps, and will rend the caul of their *hearts* (לִבָּם)."

Nah. 2 7, "Her maids shall lead her as with the voice of doves, tabering upon their *breasts* (לִבְבֵהֶן, *hearts*)."

That the sacred writers do recognize the heart in its physiological character as the central organ of the system, is evident from that metaphorical use of the term by which it is applied to designate the *middle, midst,* or *inner part* of any thing, as of the sea, the heavens, &c. Thus,

Ex. 15. 8, "The depths were congealed in the *heart* (לֵב) of the sea."

2 Sam. 18. 14, "And he took three darts in his hand, and thrust them through the *heart* (לֵב) of Absalom while he was yet alive in the *midst* (לֵב) of the oak," i. e. of the oak-forest.

Deut. 4. 11, "And the mountain burned with fire unto the *midst* (לֵב) of heaven." So καρδία τῆς γῆς, *heart of the earth,* Mat 12 40

Ezek. 27. 25, "Thou wast made very glorious in the *midst* (לֵב, *heart*) of the seas."

Mat. 12 40, "As Jonas was three days and three nights in

the whale's belly; so shall the Son of man be three days and three nights in the *heart* (καρδίᾳ) of the earth."

The instances now given are the principal which the Scriptures afford of the primary or physical sense of the term *heart*. We now come to the vastly larger list of specimens of its secondary or tropical sense in reference to the *rational* and *sensitive* principles of our nature, in which it remarkably accords with the Latin usage of *cor* in the phrase *vir cordatus, a man of heart,* i. e. *an intelligent man, a man of understanding.* Of these we propose to give only a sufficient number to illustrate clearly the usage.

§ 2.

לֵב or לֵבָב *in the sense of Mind, Understanding, Wisdom, the Faculty of Thinking, &c.*

1. *Spoken of man.*

Gen. 6. 5, "And God saw . . . that every imagination of the thoughts of *his heart* (לִבּוֹ) was only evil continually."

" 31. 26, "What hast thou done that thou hast stolen away *unawares* to me (לְבָבִי—Lit. stolen from *my heart*)," i. e. while I was unaware of it.

" 24. 45, "Before I had done speaking in *my heart* (לִבִּי)," i. e. in *my mind.*

Ex. 28. 3, "And thou shalt speak unto all that are *wise-hearted* (חַכְמֵי לֵב, *wise of heart*), whom I have filled with the spirit of wisdom."

Num 16. 28, "Ye shall know that the Lord hath sent me to do all these works; for I have not done them of *my own mind* (לִבִּי, *heart*)."

1 Kings, 3. 9, "Give therefore thy servant an understanding *heart* (לֵב)."

Neh. 5. 7, "Then I consulted *with myself* (לִבִּי, *my heart* consulted)."

Job, 34. 10, "Therefore hearken unto me, ye *men of understanding* (אַנְשֵׁי לֵב, *men of heart, viri cordati*)."

Prov. 7 7, "I discerned among the youths a young man void of *understanding* (לֵב, *heart*)."
" 9. 4, "As for him that wanteth *understanding* (לֵב), she saith to him," &c
" 12. 11, "He that followeth vain persons is void of *understanding* (לֵב)."
" 19. 8, "He that getteth *wisdom* (לֵב, *heart*) loveth his own soul."
" 24. 32, "When I saw and *considered it well* (אָשִׁית לִבִּי, *set my heart* upon it)."
Eccl. 9. 1, "For all this I considered in *my heart* (לְבִּי) to declare all this."
" 10. 3, "When he that is a fool walketh in the way *his wisdom* (לִבּוֹ, *his heart*) faileth him."
Is. 10. 7, "Neither doth *his heart* (לְבָבוֹ) think so; but it is in his *heart* (לְבָבוֹ) to destroy."
Dan. 4. 16, "Let his *heart* (לְבָב) be changed from man's, and let a beast's *heart* (לְבַב) be given unto him."
Hos. 7. 11, "Ephraim is like a silly dove without *heart* (לֵב)," i. e. without wisdom or discretion.

2. *Spoken of God.*
Gen 8. 21, "The Lord said in his *heart* (לִבּוֹ)," i. e. in *his mind.*
1 Kings, 9. 3, "I have hallowed this house, which thou hast built, to put my name there for ever; and mine eyes and mine *heart* (לִבִּי) shall be there for ever."
Job, 7. 17, "What is man that thou shouldst magnify him? and that thou shouldst set *thine heart* (לִבֶּךָ) upon him?" i. e. make him the object of thy thoughts. So also ch. 34. 14.
" 9. 4, "He is wise in *heart* (לֵב) and mighty in strength."
" 36. 5, "He is mighty in strength and *wisdom* (לֵב, *heart*)."
Jer 7. 31, "Which I commanded them not, neither came it into *my heart* (וְלִבִּי)."

USAGE OF לֵב, καρδία, HEART.   105

§ 3

לֵב or לֵבָב *as denoting the Principle which is the Seat and Subject of Sensations, Feelings, Emotions, and Passions of various kinds, as Love, Joy, Confidence, Hope, Hatred, Contempt, Sorrow, Despair, &c.*

The instances under this head are by far more numerous than any other, and are entirely equivalent to those we have already cited under the preceding terms נֶפֶשׁ and רוּחַ. We barely present a sufficient number to serve as a specimen of the whole.

Ex. 4. 14, " He will be glad in his *heart* (לִבּוֹ)."
" 7. 3, "I will harden Pharaoh's *heart* (לֵב)." So often elsewhere.
" 35. 5, " Whosoever is of a willing *heart* (לֵב)."
" 35. 21, " Every one whose *heart* (לֵב) stirred him up."
Num 32. 9, " They discouraged the *heart* (לֵב) of the children of Israel."
Deut. 28. 6, " The Lord shall give thee a trembling of *heart* (לֵב) and failing of eyes."
Judg. 16. 25, " And it came to pass when their *hearts* (לִבָּם) were merry."
1 Sam. 2. 1, " *My heart* (לִבִּי) rejoiceth in the Lord."
2 Sam. 15. 6, " Absalom stole the *hearts* (לְבוּת) of the men of Israel."
1 Kings, 21. 7, " Let thine *heart* (לִבְּךָ) be merry."
1 Chron. 15. 29, " She despised him in her *heart* (לִבָּהּ) "
2 Chron. 29. 31, " As many as were of a free *heart* (לֵב)."
Job, 31. 7, " *Mine heart* (לִבִּי) walked after mine eyes."
Ps. 34. 18, " The Lord is nigh unto them that are of a broken *heart* (לֵב)."
" 105. 25, " He turned their *hearts* (לִבָּם) to hate his people "
Prov. 11. 20, " They that are of a froward *heart* (לֵב) are abomination to the Lord "

6

Prov. 22. 11, "He that loveth pureness of *heart* (לֵב)"

" 26. 23, "Burning lips and a wicked *heart* (לֵב) are like a potsherd covered with silver dross."

Eccl. 11. 10, "Therefore remove sorrow from *thy heart* (לִבְּךָ), and put away evil from thy flesh"

Jer. 17. 9, "The *heart* (לֵב) is deceitful above all things."

Ezek. 13. 32, "Ye have made the *heart* (לֵב) of the righteous sad."

" 28. 17, "*Thine heart* (לִבְּךָ) was lifted up."

Hos. 2. 14, "I will allure her, and bring her into the wilderness, and speak *comfortably unto her* (עַל לִבָּהּ, *to her heart*)."

" 11. 8, "*Mine heart* (לִבִּי) is turned within me."

Am. 2. 16, "He that is *courageous* (אַמִּיץ לִבּוֹ, *strong of his heart*) among the mighty shall flee away naked in that day."

Obad. 3, "The pride of *thine heart* (לִבְּךָ) hath deceived thee."

Zech. 7. 12, "They made their *hearts* (לִבָּם) as an adamant stone."

Mal. 4. 6, "He shall turn the *heart* (לֵב) of the fathers to the children, and the *heart* (לֵב) of the children to their fathers." Comp. Luke, 1. 17.

Mat. 5. 8, "Blessed are the pure in *heart* (καρδία)"

" 11. 29, "Learn of me, for I am meek and lowly in *heart* (καρδία)."

Mark, 16. 14, "He upbraided them with hardness of *heart* (καρδίας)."

John, 13. 2, "The devil having put into the *heart* (καρδίαν) of Judas Iscariot to betray him."

Acts, 2. 46, "Did eat their meat with gladness and singleness of *heart* (καρδίας)."

Rom. 2. 5, "But after thy hardness and impenitent *heart* (καρδίαν), treasurest up unto thyself wrath."

2 Cor. 2. 4, "Out of much anguish of *heart* (καρδίας) I wrote you," &c.

Eph. 6. 22. "That he might comfort your *hearts* (καρδίας)"

CHAPTER VI.

General Results.

The reader has now had arrayed before him the evidence on which a judgment is to be formed of the Scriptural import of the word *soul*, and consequently of the degree to which it acquaints us with the true and essential nature of that part of our being. He has seen that the usage is, in many respects, peculiar, the original term (ψυχή) sometimes conveying the import of *breath*, sometimes of *life*, sometimes of the principle which *thinks* and *feels*, sometimes of the *person* in general, and in some few cases of the *dead body*. The chain of relation or filiation by which these senses grow out of each other, can perhaps be traced without much difficulty in regard to most of them; but as to the last, it does indeed present a very remarkable apparent solecism, that the word which, in its dominant usage, designates the *soul* in contradistinction from the *body*, should be used in any case to denote the *body* itself whether viewed as living or dead. We have given, however, under its appropriate head, the only solution of the problem that we are prepared to suggest, viz., that the term ordinarily employed to designate the principle which mainly constitutes man, man, while he lives, and the existence of which is only assured to the senses by the *body* which it animates, is used to denominate the *body* after death. The usage is evidently founded upon the assumption that *the soul is the true and essential man*, and though this man here inhabits a gross material body through which his existence and properties are manifested, yet this body is a mere adventitious appendage to his essential entity, one which he lays aside at death, and which being forsaken leaves him still a perfect personal human being, as much so as the laying aside of his garments at night

If then the question be asked, which of all these various senses is to be fixed upon as leading and paramount, we do not hesitate to answer, that of *person*. In other words, the *soul* is that principle in man which constitutes his *true personality*, and this is but another form of saying, that *the soul is the man himself as a living, thinking, feeling, active being.* We think it will unquestionably appear, upon a recurrence to the illustrations given above of the various usages of the term, that they easily resolve themselves into the *prevailing* sense of *person*, indicating that *a man's soul is himself.** This is clearly the import of a multitude of passages where the term is rendered *life*. Thus, "He that keepeth his mouth keepeth his *life*," i. e. himself. "The Son of man came to give his *life* a ransom for many," i e. to give himself. "Have wrought falsehood against *my own life*," i e. against myself. "God do so to me, and more also, if Adonijah have not spoken this against *his own life*," i. e. against himself. Let it be remembered that in these and other similar instances the original is the identical word which in our language is represented by *soul*. The verbal distinction of *life* and *soul* so familiar to us is not known in the Hebrew.

Viewed in this light the *usus loquendi* as displayed under ch. I. § 7, (p. 56,) cannot but strike the reader as very remarkable. There we find numerous instances like the following: "And he requested *for himself* (לְנַפְשׁוֹ, *for his soul*) that he might die." "Ye shall not make *yourselves* (נַפְשֹׁתֵיכֶם, *your souls*) abominable." "Neither shall ye de-

---

* Mr Barnes, in commenting on Job, 33 18, "He keepeth back his soul from the pit," remarks, "The word *soul* in the Heb is often equivalent to *self*, and the idea is, that he keeps *the man* from the pit in this manner." So again in v 22, of the same chapter, "His soul draweth near unto the grave,"—"that is, he himself dies, for the word *soul* is often used to denote *self*"

file *yourselves* (נַפְשֹׁתֵיכֶם, *your souls*)." "To bind *his soul* with a bond," i. e. to bind himself. "The Lord hath sworn by *himself* (בְּנַפְשׁוֹ, *by his soul*)" "Think not with *thyself* (בְּנַפְשֵׁךְ, *with thy soul*)." "He teareth *himself* (נַפְשׁוֹ, *his soul*) in his anger." So the "losing one's *soul*," Mat. 10. 30, is distinctly paralleled by "losing one's *self*," John, 12. 25. This form of diction is very frequent in the renderings of the cognate Syriac and Arabic. Thus, Mat. 28. 6, "And he departed and hanged *himself*." Syr. "Hanged *his soul*." Heb. 10 12, "*By his own blood* he entered in once into the holy place." Syr. "By the blood of *his soul*." Gal. 1. 4, "Who gave *himself* for our sins." Arab. "Who gave *his soul*" Gal. 2. 20, "Who loved me and gave *himself* for me." Arab. "Gave *his soul* for me." John, 21. 17, "When thou wast young thou girdedst *thyself*" Syr. "Thou girdedst *thy soul*." Lev. 19 18, "Thou shalt love thy neighbor *as thyself*" Syr. "As *thy soul*." Jer. 3. 11, "The backsliding Israel hath justified *herself* more than treacherous Judah." Heb. and Syr. "Hath justified *her soul*." The same usage is to be recognized in the following passages from the apocryphal book of the son of Syrach, or Ecclesiasticus ch. 2. 1, "Prepare thy *soul* (ψυχήν) for temptation," i. e. prepare *thyself*. Ch. 29. 19, "Forget not thy surety, for he has given his *life* (ψυχήν) for thee," i. e. hath given *himself*. Ch. 37. 7, "From a counsellor guard *thy soul* (τὴν ψυχήν σου)," i. e. guard thyself.

We see not what room can remain for doubt, that the dominant usage of the term *soul* in the sacred writers makes it equivalent to a *man's self*, and the great question now before us is the question of Scriptural usage. If then a man's *soul is himself*, even in the present life, and yet it is the *soul* which exists after death, is it not inevitable that we must carry the same fulness of import into the usage of the term in its relation to the *soul* as translated from the body into the world of spirits? The meaning of the word *soul* must be commensurate with the real truth of man's nature as man. If we can satisfy ourselves, on competent grounds, of the true constitutive elements of our being apart from the body, then we virtually attain to a correct definition of the term *soul*. Now it is clear, from what has been advanced above, that besides the body there enters into the constitution of our nature the two distinct elements denominated $\psi v \chi \acute{\eta}$ and $\pi v \tilde{\epsilon} \tilde{v} \mu \alpha$. These both live after death, and live together. Yet in ordinary parlance it is usual to say that the *soul* lives when the *body* dies. The *soul* therefore cannot be a monad, a simple uncompounded substance, but the term must be understood as representing the complex idea of $\psi v \chi \acute{\eta}$ and $\pi v \tilde{\epsilon} \tilde{v} \mu \alpha$, and this notwithstanding that *soul* is, in a multitude of cases, in actual usage, applied as a designation of the first of these principles in contradistinction from the second. It seems therefore essential to the just idea of the *soul*, as a term indicative of the future *man*, that it should embrace both these elements of existence, and we have already given our reasons for believing that the former stands to the latter in the relation of a *vehiculum* or *body*. It is no objection to this that we are wholly incompetent to disclose the *inner essence* of this principle and show *how* it is that it performs this office. Nothing in the scope or design of the present essay imposes upon us the responsibility of penetrating into the hidden recesses of our being and defining what our faculties cannot grasp. The true question is a question relating to the inferences to be drawn from certain *facts* which are admitted on every other theory as well as on our own. These facts are, that Scriptural usage makes clearly the distinction which we affirm, and that physiology as clearly recognizes it. For as it is obvious that the *body*, as such, is not the subject of *sensation*, this power must inhere in the $\psi v \chi \acute{\eta}$, which forsakes the body at death, and which can never be proved to have lost its *sensitive* attributes by such a change of relation. The whole force of the evidence bears in the contrary direction. As the $\psi v \chi \acute{\eta}$, during the life of the body, is the true seat and subject of what are ordinarily termed *bodily sensations,* so we deem the presumption perfectly legitimate, that it remains such when the body is abandoned. What else can be inferred when once it is admitted that the *body* is not truly the subject of *sensation,* as it certainly is not of *thought* ? It is the interior man inhabiting the body that sees, hears, touches, tastes, smells. This power is indeed lost to the body when the soul forsakes it. But is it lost to the *soul?* Can we conceive of a human soul departing in its full integrity from its earthly tenement, and yet leaving behind it or losing in its exit those distinguishing properties which went to constitute it what it was during its connexion with the body? What adequate idea can we form of the disembodied *man,* if we suppose him, after death, to be an entity incapable of sensation? Admit that in the present life sensation is effected only by means of the senses; yet the senses are not themselves the sentient. The eye does not see—the ear does not hear—the hand does not touch—though it is true that they are respectively the *mediums* through which the interior *power* of sensation acts, and this *power,* we contend, is essential to the integrity of the soul or the man, and must go with him where he goes, and abide with him where he abides. We cannot conceive of the perfect man without it.*

If then it be conceded that the bodily senses are the mere organical functionaries of an intelligent percipient power or principle throned within, we say that the conclusion bears down upon us with commanding urgency, that what man is substantially here, that he is substantially here-

* " No man can show it to be impossible to the Supreme Being to have given us the power of perceiving external objects without such organs We have reason to believe that when we put off these bodies, and all the organs belonging to them, our perceptive powers shall rather be improved than destroyed or impaired "—*Reid's Essay on the Organs of Sense,* ch I

after. Must it not be so? Look at the phenomena of death. There is the eye in its perfect integrity, but it does not see. There is the ear in all the completeness of its mechanism, but it does not hear. There is the wondrous apparatus of nerves spread over the whole surface of the body, but it has no feeling. The seeing, hearing, feeling power or *person* has gone. The house remains, but the occupant has departed. Yet consider what powers, what faculties, what thoughts, what memories, what affections were comprised within the limits of that existence which had just before animated this living, moving, acting mass! Has that perished? Was it not the true man—the actual person in all his distinguishing attributes—which has now passed out of sight? That which is left behind, though it was all that was visible to the senses, was the mere temporary envelope of the indwelling spirit, and we never call it *the man*. It is now *the corpse*, and we speak of it, not as *he*, but *it*. We lay *it* out, we deposit *it* in the grave, we say that *it* turns to corruption. But *the man*, with all his distinctive attributes—his varied powers of thought, affection, and will—his true personality and character—survives this dislodgment from the earthly house, and goes in all his integrity into another sphere of being, where he lives subject to the same moral and intellectual laws that governed his existence here. *The soul is the man.*

Thus far we have seen how remarkably the results of our philological inductions agree with those of physiological science. But we have still more decisive testimony on this head. The narrative of the Apostle, 2 Cor. 12. 1–4, is an invaluable item of Revelation simply on the score of pneumatology. In that he informs that *he* was caught up to the third heaven and heard unutterable things which it was not lawful (i. e. possible) to utter, and yet he informs us that during the time he " knew not whether he was in the body, or out of the body," thus proving the intrinsic possibility of translation to a state in which the subject shall possess the power of *hearing* while the material organs of this sense are in abeyance. Was it not the true *person* of Paul that was now for a time transferred to the spiritual world, and was he not in full possession of the power of sensation relative to the objects of that world?

The same truth is taught us by our Lord's words to the dying thief: "Verily I say unto thee, this day shalt thou be with me in paradise." *Thou*—assuredly a designation of the *person*, for his body was to remain suspended on the cross. This *person* is denoted in Scripture language by *the soul*, which therefore is of necessity tantamount to all that we are naturally forced to understand as constituting the *integrity of the man*.*

It may now be asked how the common doctrine of the Resurrection can be made to consist with the view above

---

* We insert the following impressive extract in the hope that attention may be called to the volume of beautiful and profound Essays from which it is taken.

"Into the spirit-world man enters at death. While in this lower world his spiritual body was within his natural body, giving it life, and power, and sense. It was always his spiritual eye which saw, his spiritual ear which heard, his spiritual senses which took cognizance of all things about him. But while he lived in the material body, it was only through the material organs of that body, that the eye of his spiritual body could see and its ear could hear; and for that purpose these natural organs were exquisitely fitted to the spiritual organs, which they served as instruments. But when these material organs or coverings fall off, the spiritual eye, the true and living eye, does not lose the power of seeing. It loses the power of seeing the material things for which it once possessed a material organ, and acquires the power of seeing the spiritual substances and forms which this material organ had veiled. So it is with all the senses and all the organs of the body. The man *rises* from that portion of earth which his soul once vivified; *rises* with the spiritual body he always had, and *rises* in full possession of all his senses and faculties, into a world of spiritual substances, of which his spiritual senses and organs now take cognizance in the same manner as the material organs here perceive material things. In a word, Death is Birth, and there a man rises as before, but in a new world, yet with all his organs, limbs, senses, faculties."—*Essays by Theophilus Parsons, Jr.*, p. 30.

presented of the Scriptural usage of the terms in question? Is any thing wanting to our process of proof that the term *soul* really denotes the *spiritual man* and consequently implies all that can fairly be understood of the *spiritual body?* But the *spiritual body* is the *body of the resurrection*. Is this twofold? Is a spiritual body, which is to be prepared from the material relics of the present body, and to be forthcoming at the " end of the world," to be *added* to the spiritual body, which is truly indicated by the word *soul*, and which the righteous immediately assume at death?* . We demand a candid and unequivocating reply to this interrogatory. It is plain that it can be answered in the affirmative only by denying the soundness of the whole train of exegesis embodied in the foregoing pages; and if this be denied we claim to be informed what *is* the sense of the terms brought

---

* The incongruity of the common view on this subject will appear still more palpable if it be borne in mind, that in the order of the divine economy it is the ψυχη which really elaborates, by its inherent laws, the material body inhabited in the present life To suppose then that the old body shall be raised and made to reclothe the separated spirit—waiving at present the insuperable difficulties which attend the supposition—is to suppose a complete inversion of the established mode of God's operation It is to suppose a body superinduced upon the ψυχη, which the ψυχη had no agency in forming, and this to our thought is very much like the idea of the shell of an egg being superinduced upon the contents of the egg after they are all perfectly formed The *order* of creation is that they shall be formed together But is the Deity, it will be asked, *restricted* to the observance of his own laws? Does he not reserve to himself the right of miraculous interpositions when he sees fit? Undoubtedly he does, whenever a competent *reason* weighs with him to that effect. Here then the only question will be as to the fact of such a *reason*. Others may believe that it exists; we do not We believe that the conditions of man's being in every stage of it are the result of fixed laws, and that there is nothing more truly miraculous in regard to man's assumption of the spiritual body, than there is in regard to his assumption of the natural body But if one does not adopt this view *without* reasoning, it is not probable that he ever will *with* it. It is the fruit of a sentiment rather than of an argument

under review ? What is meant by the $\psi v \chi \dot{\eta}$, in what respects does it differ from the $\pi v \epsilon \tilde{v} \mu \alpha$, and how is the *psychical* principle of beasts distinguished from that of man ? It must be seen by the light of a half-opened eye, that not merely negative but affirmative ground must be taken by the opponent of the views here maintained. If we have given an erroneous exhibition of the actual usage of the sacred writers in their application of these terms, or if we have drawn from it unwarranted inferences, let the fallacy of our reasoning be *exposed*, and not barely *denounced* as uprooting all established ideas of the true teaching of holy writ. We profess to have treated the subject in a legitimate and scholarlike manner, with the sole aim of attaining the *truth* involved in it. Let the argument be met in the same manner and in the same spirit. We have but the one object, common to all reverent and honest minds, to compass the true sense of the inspired oracles on a point of transcendent moment to every believer in the divinity of those oracles. It is possible that we may have erred in our interpretations, and he that shall show this, upon adequate grounds, will find his draft duly honored upon the profoundest gratitude of our heart. For the present we confess we see not what link is lacking in the chain of proof of our main conclusion, or what flaw there is in any of the links not lacking.

We hold it to be unquestionable, that as a fact of general Scriptural usage, the term נפש$=\psi v \chi \dot{\eta}=soul$ is employed by the sacred writers to denote the *internal man* in contradistinction from the body which he inhabits. But the same term is applied also to the beasts, from which it is evident that they possess the principle denominated $\psi v \chi \dot{\eta}$ in common with man; yet it is not supposed that the beasts are immortal. The immortality of man, therefore, is based upon some other principle than the $\psi v \chi \dot{\eta}$, and consequently we are forced upon the conviction that the $\psi v \chi \dot{\eta}$ after death does not constitute the entireness of his being. In conjunction with the $\psi v \chi \dot{\eta}$ there must exist a higher essence which shall be to it what the soul is usually understood to be to the body. We have already seen that in the economy of the corporeal structure the *sensations* pertain not to the body, but to the *sensitive principle* which lives in the body, and with which the inner spiritual essence more immediately communicates. But the ψυχή is the *sensitive principle,* and constitutes undoubtedly the material of that exquisite apparatus by means of which the body *is said* to feel. The ψυχή, moreover, we are taught to regard as the grand intermediate agent in what are termed the *vital functions*, which we enjoy in common with the lower animals, and, in a still inferior degree, with the vegetable world. Of the intrinsic nature of this ψυχή we are ignorant; and to the question whether it be *material* or *immaterial* we are unable to return an answer, because we know no more of the intrinsic nature of matter than of that of spirit.*

---

* "The question respecting the *internal nature*," says Knapp, "and the *quality* of the human soul, is one of those difficult and obscure questions which can never be satisfactorily answered in the present life. It cannot certainly be decided by any thing in the Bible. The soul is there merely contrasted with the body (בָּשָׂר, *flesh*). The latter, we are informed, will return to the earth from which God created it, and the former will return to God *who gave it*, i. e. produced it in a different way from the body. So much is perfectly evident, that the Bible always distinguishes between the soul and body as different substances, and ascribes to each peculiar properties and operations; and this is in full accordance with the manner in which this subject was understood and represented in all the ancient world.

"We should mistake very much, however, if we should suppose that the ancient Israelites, merely because they distinguished widely between soul and body, possessed those strict metaphysical ideas of the *spirituality* or *immateriality* of the soul, which are prevalent in the modern schools of philosophy. Such ideas are by far too refined and transcendent to belong to that age; as are also the pure metaphysical ideas of God, which now prevail. . The notion of the ancient world respecting *spirit* was by no means the same with that of our modern metaphysicians. And if the question of the perfect immateriality of the soul had been left to them, and theologians had stopped where the Bible does, and omitted those inquiries, the object of which lies far beyond their sphere, they would

But whatever be its *nature*, we infer its *office* hereafter from what we know to be its office here. Pervading, informing, animating during life every part of the corporeal structure, just as the water fills and saturates all the pores of the dripping sponge, the ψυχή is still but the *receptacle* of that higher *spiritual* principle which acts directly upon it, as the steam acts upon the iron enginery of the boat. The machinery is the true body to the steam which sets it in motion But the steam and the machinery can exist apart from all connexion with the framework of the boat in mutual relation to each other, and so the ψυχή and the πνεῦμα—the *soul* and the *spirit*—can and do exist separate from the body which they energize on earth, and, thus existing, why is not the one the *body* to the other? What but the union of the two principles constitutes the *real man* of the other life? And here we are not to suffer the force of the evidence to be vacated by the difficulty of predicating *body* of that

---

have done wisely This doctrine respecting the *immateriality* of the soul, in the strict philosophical sense of the term, is of far less consequence to their religion than is commonally supposed The reason why so much importance has been supposed to attach to this doctrine is, that it was considered as essential to the metaphysical proof of the *immortality* of the soul. But since the immateriality of the soul, in the strictest sense, can never be made fully and obviously certain, whatever philosophical arguments may be urged in its favor, the proof of *immortality* should not be built upon it Nor were the fine-spun theories of immaterialism ever resorted to by theologians to prove the immortality of the soul, or ascribed by them to the Bible, until Hobbes, Toland, De la Mettrie, and other materialists, had so perverted the doctrine of materialism, as to deduce from it the destructibility of the soul, or its annihilation at the death of the body But in truth, the immortality of the soul does neither depend for proof upon its immateriality, nor can be certainly deduced from it It is possible for one to doubt whether the strict immateriality of the soul can be proved, and yet to be convinced of its immortality The strongest advocates of immateriality must allow that God *might* annihilate a spirit, however simple its nature might be. Why then, on the other hand, *might* he not make a substance not entirely simple, immortal?—*Christian Theology*, Vol II, p 372-74

which comes not under the usual conditions of matter, and sustains not the usual relation of material substances to *space*. We do not refuse to acknowledge the possession by angels of some kind of *bodies* What greater difficulty in conceiving the same endowment in regard to translated human beings?*

---

* "'THERE IS A SPIRITUAL BODY' It is then *body*, and not mere *spirit*, to which the reasoning of the apostle relates He is treating of the transition which human nature is destined to pass through from one condition of corporeal existence to another, and he speaks of the laying down a body that is gross or at least infirm, perishable, and ignoble, and the taking up a body that shall be potent, illustrious and permanent .
That which Christianity requires us to believe is the actual survivance of our personal consciousness *embodied*, and the perpetuity of our sense of good and evil, and our continued sensibility of pain and pleasure, and the unbroken recollection, in another life, of the events and affections of another state What Christianity affirms is, that the LIFE—moral, intellectual, and active or corporeal—is not commensurate with, or dependent upon, animal organization; but that it may and that it will spring up anew from the ruins of its present habitation. 'Destroy *this* body,' and the man still lives but whether he might live immaterially is a mere question of philosophy which the inspired writers do not care to decide In almost all instances it is with facts, rather than with abstruse principles, that they have to do; and in relation to our present subject, after having peremptorily affirmed that human nature is to survive in another state, and is to rise embodied from the ashes of its present animal organization, St Paul leaves speculation at large, neither denying nor affirming any hypothesis that may consist with the fact which alone is important to our religious belief, (the fact, viz, that man lives after death *in a body*.)

"Let it then be distinctly kept in view, that although the essential independence of mind and matter, or the *abstract possibility* of the former existing apart from corporeal life, may well be considered as implied in the Christian scheme, yet an *actual* incorporeal state of the human soul, at any period of its course, is not necessarily involved in the principles of our faith, any more than it is explicitly asserted This doctrine concerning what is called the immateriality of the soul should ever be treated as a merely philosophical speculation, and as unimportant to our Christian profession The question concerning pure immateriality, we regard as having been passed untouched, by St Paul; nor do we consider it as in any specific manner important to the inquiries upon which we are about to enter"—*Physical Theory of Another Life,* p, 15

There can be no doubt, however, that our ideas on this subject become inadequate and confused, from the fact that the distinction which we have intimated as subsisting between what we term the *psychical* and *spiritual* elements of our nature is not clearly recognized in the *prevailing* diction of the sacred writers. They speak of the *soul* or *inner man* as a one, as a simple, just as they often speak of the outer man, or that man which in this life we know to be composed of body and mind. They leave the *verity of our being* to be discovered by such researches and inductions as constitute the province of anthropology, guided by a comparison of *all* the forms of speech which the Scriptures themselves afford. From these sources we learn that the above distinction must necessarily be made, and consequently that the *soul*, in this sense, is in fact a complex, the analysis of which leaves us with the inference that man's *spirit* departs from the body of flesh clothed with a *psychical* body, which in common parlance is termed *spiritual*, not from its essential nature, but from its superadded character. This, we conceive, develops to us the true theory of the resurrection, and the conclusion can only be denied by denying the justness of the premises.

It is for the physiologist to discover, if he can, the intrinsic qualities of the $\psi\nu\chi\dot{\eta}$ and the *modus operandi* of its organific powers. This is by no means incumbent on him who professes simply to establish the *facts* of the inspired verbal usage which obtains in regard to the general theme. We may say, however, on this head, that the phenomena of the vital processes, of sensation, digestion, and nutrition, do unquestionably connect themselves with the aerial, electrical, and galvanic agencies which are incessantly at work around us and within us, and that in some way, at present unknown to us, the *psychical* element of man enters into the closest relation with these invisible substances. The assertion of this fact amounts not to the position that *life* is *identical* with any of them, nor does it afford any just ground for a carping cavillation, as if really propounding a wild and visionary theory of a *spiritual* body constructed of *material* elements. We advance no theory on the subject. We know nothing of the internal essence of matter We recognize simply the existence of certain *facts* in physical science which no man can deny without publishing an affidavit of his own ignorance, and these *facts* we place by the side of certain scriptural formulas of speech, and call upon the reader to collate their respective testimony to the truth and soundness of the conclusions we draw from them. The great question to be decided is, whether the language of Scripture on the subject before us conveys an *absolute truth*. Do the terms employed compel us to recognize in man's psychological constitution another principle in addition to the $\psi v \chi \eta$? If they do, have we rightly stated the distinction ? The demand cannot be unreasonable, that the error should be clearly pointed out, and especially that the relation which these two elements sustain to each other should be definitely disclosed

The bearing of the whole discussion thus far pursued on the doctrine of the Resurrection cannot but be perceived at a glance. If the train of reasoning now presented be sound, the inference would seem to follow irresistibly that we have found the resurrection-body in the soul itself But if the resurrection-body be a spiritual body, and if such a body, as we have defined it, be involved, in the nature of the case, in the *soul*, we cannot but inquire what are the grounds for anticipating the resuscitation of the old, decayed, dissipated, and vanished body of flesh ? Even if it should be recalled from the vasty deep of past existences, and should come forth at the divine bidding, still what end is to be answered by it ? Is the first spiritual body with which the spirit enters the world of spirits to be laid aside, and a second spiritual body, constructed of the materials of the fleshly body, to be substituted in its place ? If so, where is the scriptural evidence of the fact ? Or is the second spiritual corporeity to be *added* to the first? If so, where, again, is the evidence of this? If it be admitted—what we contend cannot be consistently denied—that the *soul* necessarily supposes a body, then the belief of the assumption of *another* body must rest upon the anticipation, and this upon the divine declaration, of some great and stupendous change in the conditions and relations of our being at the period when it is supposed to occur. If there is to be no essential change of condition or relation, it seems difficult to conceive a reason for the laying aside of one spiritual body and the assumption of another, or for the addition of one to another, even granting that either could reasonably come within the range of our thoughts. If there is to be such a marked crisis in the future lot of man, as to warrant the theory of the resumption of the former body, whatever transforming or spiritualizing process it may undergo, it would seem necessary to suppose it one that should involve a transfer of departed spirits to some new sphere of existence; for if they pass into the world of spirits with bodies adapted to that world, why should we suppose any change as long as they remain there?

But on this point we are ready at once to take the position, that the Scriptures, rightly interpreted, give no intimation of any such transfer, nor, consequently, of any such corresponding bodily change. If such an event is in prospect, it must be at what is termed the "end of the world," to which the prevalent notions of the Christian world assign the so called general resurrection, general judgment, second personal advent of Christ, &c.. But a stricter exegesis of the inspired language, which we have attempted in the work on the Resurrection, dissipates the basis on which such an expectation rests, and resolves the various proof-texts into the enunciation of a spiritual process of the divine administration which is even now going on.

As to the idea, more or less current among good men, that the globe which we now inhabit is to be in some way subjected to the action of a purgatorial fire, which is to transmute and purify and sublimate its substance so as to render it a fit abode for the risen righteous, we know not of a single passage in the compass of revelation which can be fairly construed in support of that theory. As we have elsewhere remarked, "The language of holy writ is unequivocal, that the bodies of the resurrection are *spiritual*, and how can spiritual bodies inhabit a material earth? The two things we scruple not to pronounce incompatible with each other, as far as human reason is competent to form a judgment. The material world was made for men possessed of material bodies, and the spiritual world for spiritual beings, and from the spiritual world we of course exclude all our ordinary ideas of matter. The saints enter into ' houses not made with hands *eternal in the heavens*' No intimation is given of their being transferred to earth. We do not deny that there may be a *communication* between these two worlds. The glorified dwellers in the heavenly sphere may honor with their visits the humbler inmates of the terrestrial mansions, as angels have often done in ages past, but we still affirm that neither reason nor revelation gives any countenance to the conceit that the beatified hosts of heaven, with Abraham, Isaac, and Jacob—with patriarchs and prophets—are, at any period of time or eternity, to sojourn for permanence in these terraqueous abodes Heaven is the place for the spirits of just men made perfect, and heaven alone Every class of beings is adapted to the element in which it is designed to live. Neither bodiless spirits nor spiritualized bodies are adapted to the element of earth on which our bodies of flesh and blood reside " (*Nebuchadnezzar's Vision*, p 131.)

If then the scriptural evidence of any such future change is entirely lacking, what grounds exist for the belief that it will ever occur, or that the spiritual bodies which we assume at death will *ever* be superseded or laid aside ? What adequate *reason*, then, have we for the expectation, that the decomposed and dispersed fabrics of our present bodies will ever be reconstructed and made a second time to invest their once tenanting spirits?

If it be said in reply that this is a subject so far transcending all the previous conceptions of the human mind, and resting so simply and entirely on the authoritative announcements of Revelation, that no inquiry is to be urged as to the *reasons* and *ends* of the sublime procedure, we at once rejoin, that God has so constituted us that we *cannot help* propounding queries on this head; especially when we find other portions of this same authoritative record abounding with intimations that force upon us conclusions directly at variance with what is deemed the most obvious import of its letter in the passages insisted upon. Does the inspired word thus speak with a divided voice? Does it require us to hold our reason in abeyance, and receive implicitly both sides of an opposite testimony? Is not the proof as clear from the citations above adduced that the good man assumes a *spiritual body* at death as it can be from any other passages that he does not receive that body for an indefinite tract of ages, and in connexion with an event which can never be shown to have been predicted? Is this apparent contrariety of the divine teaching to be piously blinked by the believer for fear he should honor philosophy at the expense of faith? For ourselves we have not so learned the oracles of truth. We find no demand made upon our reason for a suppression of its dictates in order to a due reverencing the word of inspiration. We perceive no difficulty in so interpreting the divine announcements as to bring them into harmony with our human deductions. We are conscious of no necessity to admit a construction of one part of Scripture that shall set it at war with another; and yet this is the alternative which we charge upon the common interpretation of those portions of the sacred volume which relate to the Resurrection—with how much justice we leave it to the reader to judge. We know nothing of the *presumption* often affirmed of any attempt to bring the divine procedures within the range of our intelligence. Nor can we rest satisfied with resolving into sheer omnipotence the accomplishment of results which involve ideas incompatible with each other.

Such we have found to be the amount of nearly all the argument bestowed upon the work which has given occasion to the present Essay. Thus, in one of the most stringent reviews of the " Anastasis," (*Biblic. Repos. for April*, 1845,) the author assumes to state a *common sense* view of the subject, and to draw up a declaration of his faith in the following terms: " ' I believe in the existence of God, possessing infinite intelligence and almighty power. I believe that He has revealed the future resurrection of the bodies of the dead. I believe that He has revealed it in such a way, and by the use and application of such terms and sentences, as that the most direct, natural, and obvious impression would be, that there is to be an identity of some kind between the body that dies and the one that is to be raised. As I am a common man, and not qualified either to apprehend or answer very acutely philosophical difficulties, I still further believe that the God I worship is perfectly competent to secure this identity; that He has such a sovereign control over the present destiny of elementary particles and organized masses, that whatever is necessary to be done in the premises to realize the truth of a biblical doctrine, He can and will do.' This is my creed, as a plain common Christian, compelled to interpret the Bible in its most obvious and natural sense, never having studied Greek or Hebrew; and assuming that the standard English version does not so far differ from the original text, as to create a dense cloud of *appearances* where there are no *realities*. Has the author any objection to this creed? Does it not involve philosophy enough to meet all the practical demands of a reasonable faith? We wait for an answer." p. 246.

The answer we will shortly give after adverting to some

other positions in the same article. Thus, " I now come to the point, where the philosophy of the author is entirely at issue with common sense, with what is appropriate to nature, and descriptive of things as they are. He introduces a fallacy into his own mind by the use of the word *body*, as applied to human beings. The man at seventy has changed the particles of his body ten times, and therefore has had ten different bodies. Suppose we grant the premise, the conclusion does not follow. What do we mean by *body* in this application ? We mean the organized and living *whole*, as such. The continuity of a material and vital organization, as a general aggregate—with the same inhabiting spirit—subject to the same laws of life— this is the *common*, as it is the *philosophical*, idea of the present *identity* of the body We apply the term body to the vital aggregate, as such, and if this remain, though the individual particles should change ten thousand times, it is the same body : it is, in the true and proper sense, but one body. If I should lose one of my fingers, will any man in his senses say I that have lost any portion of my identity as a body ?—If by the process of phlebotomy I should lose a pint of blood, is my identity as a body impaired ?—Not in the slightest degree, unless we are to have a new dispensation of exegesis upon the terms *body* and *identity* in this application. The author's view, that a change of particles is continually impairing the identity of the body as an organized aggregate, and giving us new bodies, carries along with it this consequence—viz, it is as difficult to admit the continuous identity of the present body in any sense, as to admit the identity of the present body and the resurrection body. His argument operates as severely on earth, as it does in eternity. And before we can admit its soundness here, we must have a new dispensation of philosophy and common sense." p 251,

So also, p. 252, " Our spontaneous self-knowledge gives us one and the same body through the whole course of our present being, in the very same sense in which it gives us a body at all. And if we may have the same knowledge in respect to identity between the present and the future body, the author may be left to play with the particles at his pleasure." And again, p. 262, "Give me an identity between the present and future body for the residence of the soul, as complete, substantial, and real, as that of my present body during successive periods, and I ask no more. And if in the latter case I may have it with an entire change of elementary particles, why may I not equally have it in the former?" Finally, he affirms the identity between the present and future body, to be one that has reference mainly to the spontaneous impressions, judgments, or cognitions of the soul (that is) to be seated in the body—an idea which he thus expands: "A man lives and dies. After death his spirit goes to the God that gave it, and his body back to the dust. At the resurrection his spirit enters into, and is united with, a spiritual body—material in one respect, but spiritual in another—a body in some respects entirely different from the one he had at death, but in other respects like it. The spontaneous impression and view of the man himself, as of those who know him, are those of *sameness*, both as to body and soul, abating the admitted but consistent differences between the present and future body. His body is the same, in this sense at least, that it is *known as such*, and is the seat of the same intelligence. Will this not give us an identity of body, substantially the very one which we have in the present life? Our bodily identity here is such mainly in reference to our intelligence, as a continuous seat of the same—such in reference to the spontaneous impressions and judgments of that intelligence —not affected by the flux and change of particles." p. 263.

Now in reference to this whole line of argument it is clear that it makes the identity between the present body and the body of the resurrection to be of the same kind with the identity of the body in successive periods in the present life, and this he resolves into an identity resting upon certain "spontaneous impressions, judgments, cognitions," &c. The fact is admitted that the body may be actually changed as to *every one* of its constituent particles several times during life—that its "atomic identity" is repeatedly lost—and yet the writer persists in maintaining, that the body is all the while the same body as an "organized aggregate," of which we are assured by "spontaneous impressions, judgments, and cognitions." Our reply to this is, that we do not admit the soundness of this sense of bodily identity, and that for the reason, that the positions assumed involve a contradiction in terms. Whatever may be our "spontaneous impressions, judgments," &c., they can never countervail the evidence of physiological facts, that the constituent particles of our present bodies do actually every one of them in process of time pass away, to be replaced by others. Consequently the whole substantial mass of our bodies is sooner or later *changed*, and that which is thus changed in the sense of one thing being substituted for another cannot in philosophical strictness still be the same. This it is superfluous to attempt to prove, because it is self-evident. I may hold a ball of snow or ice in my hand till it melts and drops into an empty bowl in the form of so much water, and I may properly say the water is the same with the snow or ice. But I cannot substitute one ball of snow for another and say either that that or the water formed from it is the same with the preceding. So in regard to the human body. It is impossible that the body which my soul inhabits to-day should be identical with the body which it inhabited ten years ago, if in the meantime every particle which then constituted it has passed away. It may indeed answer the same purpose to the soul—it may stand in the same relation to it—the "spontaneous impressions, judgments," &c., may not recognize any difference—yet the sun in the heavens is not more palpably obvious to the senses, than that the one *is* intrinsically totally different from the other. The fact is, these "spontaneous impressions," upon which the language of common parlance in reference to the subject is founded, are an entirely fallacious criterion of the truth. Our consciousness assures us only of the present possession, at each successive moment, of a body as the seat of the soul. It does not assure us of the continued identity of that body, and as the clearest demonstrations of physiology establish the fact of the perpetual flux of the component particles, it is nothing short of a downright outrage of common sense to affirm a continued identity of that which is at the same time the subject of continued change. The question in debate cannot be determined by consciousness, nor by an appeal to familiar usages of speech. It is a pure question of scientific or philosophic verity, and the true decision can be sought only at the true tribunal.

What approximation then, we ask, is made towards the truth by affirming that the identity between the buried and the risen body is the same with that which exists between the present body during successive periods? We have seen that that identity is a mere fallacy—a pure creature of the imagination. One body is here succeeded by another and a totally different body. The soul is conscious at any given period only of the body that it *now has*, but not of the process by which one has been removed and another substituted. This process we learn from other sources, yet the evidence from these sources is no less imperative than that of consciousness.* Where then is the proof that the body

---

* In contrast with the above remarks we give the following sentences from the Princeton review of the work on the " Resurrection," leaving it to the reader to judge to which view of the subject truth inclines

" It is a fact that in this life *personal* identity is never dissociated from *bodily* We carry through all the changes of the body as clear a conviction of bodily identity as of mental Sameness of body is here involved in sameness of person, and is, in this life, never separated from it Through all the processes of abstraction and accretion, incesssant in our mortal frame, no man ever yet conceived himself to have another body

of the resurrection is the *same* with the body of the present life in any of its successive stages? And if it is not the *same* as to substance, in what respect is it the same? Our critic replies, "It is the same, in this sense at least, that it is *known as such*, and is the seat of the same intelligence." Undoubtedly the future body will be *known as a body*, and it will be known too as the seat of the same intelligence. But what of that? The question is, will it be known *as the same body*—the same in substantial entity? If so, with *which* of the several successive bodies will it be identical? Here, alas! is the point where the most urgent interrogation uniformly fails to call forth any definite reply. "The reviewer is very ready to confess his want of certain knowledge as to the manner in which the relation of identity or sameness is to be established between the two bodies." But, our dear reviewer, the question between us is a question not so much as to the *manner*, as it is as to the *fact*, of such an alleged relation. Produce the evidence of the *fact*, and we will consent that you shall wave all exposition of the *manner*. And

---

And this sameness of body has nothing to do with sameness of particles. It is not a conclusion of reason, but a fact of consciousness!"

This is certainly a new office of consciousness, to testify directly contrary to known truth But what will reviewer say if we affirm, as we do, that consciousness, in the strictest propriety of speech, does not assure us of the existence of a body at all? Consciousness assures us only of what comes within the sphere of its operations, and these are *sensations, affections,* and *thoughts* It is by a subsequent process of mind that we refer our *sensations* to a body. It is indeed a process involving an infallible intuition, but it is one which transcends the office of consciousness. Yet we do not object to the use of the common language on the subject It is only when an undue advantage is taken of this language, and an attempt made to elevate it into a standard of absolute truth, that we feel called upon to enter our protest and to make the requisite philosophical discriminations So far as mere consciousness is concerned it reports a body as truly in another life as in this, for it reports merely its sensations, and these we have shown to belong to the $\psi v \chi \eta$, which lives after death

in order to give a more precise direction to your researches let us state distinctly the point which is to be *labored* in the argument. Here are some eight, ten, twelve, or twenty bodies successively tenanted by the same inhabiting soul during life. These bodies, one or all, are to be brought into a relation of *identity* with some single body affirmed to be forthcoming at the period called " the last day." We demand in the first place that you distinctly inform us whether you assume to establish the identity of any *one* of the number with the resurrection-body, or of the whole. If you take the former alternative, then we ask *which* of the plurality you fix upon, and why that one rather than any of the rest If the latter, then it is a fair requisition that you show clearly that the averments of Scripture require the belief, that the *aggregate* of all the bodies inhabited by the soul of any individual on earth shall be reproduced at the final consummation, and constitute thenceforward the residence of the soul to eternity.

We foresee at once that the solution of the problem will be referred to Omnipotence. God has expressly asserted that *the body* shall be raised, and he has infinite power to accomplish all he has announced. Therefore the body—the same body—shall be raised at the appointed time. But let it not be forgotten that the same God has endowed his creature man with an intelligence which assures him that *more than one body* inevitably enters into our conceptions of the matter, and it is utterly impossible to repress inquiry as to *the true subject* upon which his Omnipotence is to exert itself. While we are not at liberty to question for a moment the competency of infinite power to effect every thing to which it has pledged itself, we are not at the same time withheld from a humble inquisition into the terms of the proposition to which our faith is demanded. Light upon this head is all that we ask of the advocates of the common doctrine of the Resurrection. Omnipotence, it is affirmed, is engaged to accomplish *something* in respect to the resuscitation of the dead bodies of men. We simply ask to be informed what it is. We are conscious of no irreverence in propounding this query, nor do we admit that it is *unreasonably* urged upon the assertors of the common view of the doctrine. We cannot conceive that our credence is challenged to a particular doctrine of revelation but upon the ground of some *specific meaning* that is attached to the terms in which it is proposed. Our object is to ascertain this *meaning*. We have not as yet been so fortunate as to meet with any writer who has seen fit, while denying the soundness of our positions, to make any enunciation on this head that did not contrive, in some way, to evade the real point of the difficulty. By opposing an acknowledged ignorance of the *mode*, to the just demand for a clear statement of the *fact*, of an alleged relation between the present and the future body, and by falling back upon a vague resort to Omnipotence, they have uniformly managed to rid themselves of the responsibility of a categorical reply to the objections urged. Meanwhile there is no lack of intelligibility or emphasis in the language employed to characterize the presumption implied in the attempt to penetrate the cloud of darkening generalities with which the truth is so studiously enveloped. But nothing, we conceive, is eventually to be gained for the credit of Revelation by a course of proceeding which refuses to admit that the *mode* of the Resurrection is yet a *mooted point* in theology, or which would make the questioning of the received theory on that subject a virtual denial of the whole doctrine. A very slight acquaintance with the dogmatic history of the church is sufficient to evince, that conflicting views have never ceased to be entertained among divines, in regard to the mode of the fact, who have cordially received the inspired annunciation of the great and glorious fact itself.* We claim an entire freedom to discuss *in extenso* and *salva fide*

---

* See Appendix.

every thing pertaining to the Scripture disclosures of a future state, and if upon a strict exegesis of the word a sense of the language results which presents the doctrine under a new aspect, and makes the resurrection to be a resurrection, not of the *same body* at the end of the world, but of the *same person* at the end of life, we reclaim against this result's being considered as in any way undermining or impugning the essential truth which lies at the centre of the tenet, viz., *that the man who dies is to live again and possess an immortal existence in a psychical body*. This is the core of the resurrection-doctrine, and so long as this truth is held inviolate, all that is essential to the integrity of the dogma remains untouched. The retributive sanctions of the religion of Christ lose none of their force upon the view now advanced, and its accordance with the deductions of a rational psychology will have any other effect, with a liberal mind, than that of diminishing the weight of the evidence by which it is sustained. To all the impulses of the pious heart, moreover, it comes commended by the holding forth of an unbroken continuity of blissful and bodily being from the moment the eyes close in death onward through the eternal years. The comfortless theory of the sleep of the soul dies away upon this view, like the night-dream of a fevered brain when the morning beams proclaim the risen sun. The dense gloom that haunted the grave melts into glowing and genial light, and the regenerate soul awakes to a new fulness of joy in a richer assurance of the immortality that is destined to crown its hopes.

APPENDIX.

CONFLICTING VIEWS OF THE RESURRECTION.

[The following article is inserted from a pamphlet written by the Rev Augustus Clissold, a clergyman of the N J. Church, England, in answer to a Review contained in the "Preston Magazine" for Oct. 1, 1843. The portion extracted is in reply to the Reviewer's denunciation of Swedenborg's doctrine of the Resurrection, which is substantially the same with that arrived at in the present work It is, however, transferred to our pages solely with the view of presenting the historical evidence of the great diversity of opinion entertained on the subject by divines of the highest name in the Church]

'THE Reviewer says, Swedenborg states it to be the popular doctrine, that man will not live in the body after death before the last judgment; and the Reviewer adds, "This view, which is scriptural, he altogether rejects." Now, what does he reject? He rejects the doctrine that man lives in a *material* body after death, but so far from rejecting the doctrine that man lives in a spiritual body after death, the whole of this narrative maintains it, as any one may see by consulting the work.

Swedenborg exposes the folly of those who say, that departed spirits are shut up in the centre of the earth, or flying about the universe; and the Reviewer says "these notions are inventions of Swedenborg" Now, so far from these being inventions of Swedenborg, a learned writer, Suicer, maintains that the former was the opinion of St. Basil; and Lord King, in his *History of the Creed*, that it was a doctrine common among many of the early fathers it was also the opinion of Bishop Horsley, as any one may see in his Sermon upon Hades: it is the opinion of one of the most recent commentators on the Apocalypse, Mr. Govett; and both opinions are broached by Dr. Scott, whose works were printed at the Clarendon Press, Oxford. (Vol. vi. p. 43) In fine, the doctrines have been very prevalent That they are inventions of Swedenborg, is therefore an untruth.

But the Reviewer says, "the word of God represents the souls of the righteous, when absent from the body, as present with the Lord, and that to the righteous this separate state is highly desirable." We fully grant it; but why then does no less a theologian than Bishop Bull maintain, that as man is a complex of body and soul, so the body alone or the soul alone is neither of them man; that, consequently, in a separate state, the soul is only half a man, yearning for its other half? How can any person of common sense suppose that *such* a state is highly desirable? Look again to what Bishop Beveridge says in the article on the *Resurrection of Christ*. As death, he maintains, is the separation of soul and body, so after departure from this world, the soul is in a state of death as truly as the body—in a state of death, because in a state of separation—a state of which the soul is nevertheless conscious Is THIS a state highly desirable?—half a being, and that half dead, nay, more, in a state of imprisonment, and this for thousands of years! Can we suppose that, to the righteous THIS separate state is highly desirable?

But we proceed more particularly to the doctrine of the resurrection, and request your serious attention to the remarks which follow The Reviewer says, "The Scriptures at the same time, WITH ALL POSSIBLE PLAINNESS, assert that that very body which is laid in the grave, and which may for centuries moulder there, shall rise again, though in an incorruptible and very different state. Whatever inconceivable change may pass upon it, *its identity* will remain, and the body which is sown in corruption, is that which shall be raised in incorruption "

The former Magazine had said " What in the name of common sense is to be raised, if not the body? Was the soul committed to the grave?" Thus according to the writer, both common sense and Scripture assert, with all possible plainness, the resurrection of the *identical body* which is laid in the grave By the identical body which is laid in the grave, Bishop Pearson understands the same numerical body; or the same numerical collection of parts, and this he says, he holds to be a necessary and infallible truth; so that, if to this we add, that the truth is the truth of common sense, that Scripture declares it with all possible plainness, the writers doubtless conceive they are holding fast, according to St Paul, to the form of sound words which they have received. We now proceed to show from authorities in the Church of England, that so far from holding fast the words of St Paul, they are holding fast only their own opinions; so far from their being the words of St. Paul, they are the words of unskilful theologians; so far from their being sound words, they are very unsound; so far from having been received from the apostle, they have been foisted upon him; so far from their being the words of Scripture, they are nowhere to be found in Scripture.

Bishop Pearson maintains, that if the same numerical body as that deposited in the grave be not raised, it ceases to be a resurrection; for that a resurrection is the rising again of that which has fallen, and that which has fallen is the body, by being let down or deposited in the grave. Therefore, that a resurrection means a resurrection of the same numerical parts, and that any thing short of this, is not a resurrection.

Now Macknight observes, that he will not contend for the resurrection of the very numerical body; nay, that the very numerical body is not raised: and the present Bishop of London quotes the remark with approbation Mr. Hawkins, in his Bampton Lectures, will not insist upon the same numerical body, nor will Professor Lee; nor will Mr. Scott, in his Commentary on the Bible, and yet Keach maintains, with Bishop Pearson, that in order to be a resurrection, it must be a resurrection of the same numerical parts. We see then, that the necessary and infallible truth of the resurrection of the same numerical body begins to be abandoned, even by those who maintain the resurrection of the same body.

Let us next see what becomes of the doctrine of the resurrection of the same body.

The unbeliever, Thomas Paine, brought forward as a charge against the Bible, its maintaining the doctrine of the resurrection of the same body Bishop Watson answered the charge in his well known work, entitled *An Apology*. How did the Bishop publicly meet the charge? Was it by maintaining the doctrine to be a necessary and infallible truth? Was it by appealing, like other divines, to the power of Omnipotence? No such thing; but by calling upon his infidel opponent, to show that any such doctrine is contained in Scripture. The Bishop falls back upon the position of Locke, and denies with him that any such doctrine is taught by St Paul. Here, then, is a signal instance in which the doctrine, as professed by the *Preston Magazine*, shrank from before one of the most notorious infidels, and in which a Bishop of the Church of England challenges him to prove, that any such doctrine as is contained in the Magazine is contained in Scripture.

Take again, the instance of the celebrated Paley. Did Paley maintain the resurrection of the same body? On the contrary, he maintained, that the body with which we should rise, would be *totally different*—would be altered not only in quality, state, or condition, but in substance and in form. Now, how can a body totally different be one and the same? The Bishop of London admits that it cannot, and that he who maintains the body to be absolutely and totally different, cannot be said to maintain the resurrection of the same body. Thus does Paley throw aside the doctrine of the Preston Reviewer. Nay, further, so far from maintaining the resurrection of the same body to be a necessary and infallible truth, he declares the doctrine to be of no importance whatever. (Sermon 5.)

"But," says the Bishop of London, "I see no reason for departing from the doctrine of the early Church, that *we shall rise again with our bodies*, as it is asserted in the Athanasian, and implied in the Apostles' Creed; although we need not use that expression in the sense of asserting a resurrection of the same numerical collection of parts." This being the opinion of the Bishop of London, what says the late Regius Professor of Divinity at Oxford, in the learned notes to his Bampton Lectures? Dr. Burton says, "It is nowhere asserted in the New Testament, that we shall rise again with our bodies." Bishop Newton is still more decisive upon the subject. In his *Dissertation on the General Resurrection;* he observes (p. 279) · "As the corn which springeth up is not the very same seed that was sown, so thou mayest infer that the dead shall return to life, not with the same, but with other bodies than those which were buried. One would think that St. Paul had here said enough to convince any reasonable inquirer; but human curiosity will not rest so satisfied, and *the same questions are still agitated,*

APPENDIX. 137

as if the apostle had not returned any answers to them. It may be proper, therefore, more at large to explain and enforce the apostle's meaning; and the sum and substance of all may be comprised in these few words that the same persons shall rise again, but not with the same bodies, but with other bodies as it shall please God to give them," &c. Again, (p 282) "Justice requires that the same persons shall rise again, but not with the same bodies; for our bodies are not ourselves." Again, (p. 283,) "*Anastasis*, the word constantly used throughout the New Testament for the *resurrection*, signifies a rising again, a life after death, another state of the same person after the present, but never once, that I know of, signifies or even implies the resurrection of the same body." Again, (p. 287,) " St. Paul is, I think, the only one who hath treated purposely, and at large of the resurrection-body; and he is so far from defining it to be the same numerical body, that he describes it as of a totally different form and order If those who contend for the resurrection of the same body, would consider a little what it is that constitutes the same body, they would be convinced of the difficulty, or rather the impossibility, of that identical body ever rising again." Lastly, (p 292.) "What occasion is there for so many debates and controversies, so many solutions and explications of the difficulties attending the resurrection of the same body; when the Scripture proposeth no such article to our belief. * * * So far is the Scripture from asserting the resurrection of the same body, that, on the contrary, plain intimations are given that the body shall not be the same Nothing can be clearer and stronger to this purpose than the declaration of St Paul. " Thou sowest not that body that shall be "

Thus we see how the doctrine of the resurrection of the same body gradually dwindles down from a necessary infallible truth into an unscriptural dogma. Bishop Pearson maintains the resurrection of the same numerical body to be as we have said, a necessary and infallible truth. Macknight maintains the resurrection of the same body, but not the resurrection of the same numerical body. Scott maintains the resurrection of the same body, which yet he thinks will not be the same, but *alterum et idem*, another body yet the same, which Bishop Newton says is nonsense. The Bishop of London maintains the resurrection of the same body, which Paley says, nevertheless, will be totally different; upon the whole, the Bishop says, he sees no objection to the words, "we shall rise again with our bodies," a doctrine, which Dr. Burton says, is nowhere to be found in the New Testament.

And what is the history of this doctrine? Originally, in the Nicene Creed, the article was introduced of a *resurrection of the dead;* this was altered, in the Apostles' Creed to a *resurrection of the body;* this again was altered by some of the fathers, into a *resurrection of the flesh:* the Bishop of London says, this was altered again by our own Church, into the safer form of a *resurrection of the body;* and Bishop Newton intimates, it ought to be altered back again into the original form of a *resurrection of the dead;* observing, "It is earnestly to be wished that all creeds were framed, as much as may be convenient, in the words, or at least perfectly agreeable to the sense of Scripture." (p. 294, v. 6.)

And now, after the foregoing remarks, what becomes of the Reviewer's positive assertion, that "the Scriptures, *with all possible plainness*, assert that that very body which is laid in the grave, and which may for centuries moulder there, shall rise again, though in an incorruptible and very different state"? But let us proceed to another text alleged in proof of the doctrine, "The hour is coming, in which all that are in the graves shall hear his voice, and shall come forth; they that have done good to the resurrection of life, and they that have done evil to the resurrection of damnation." This text, the Reviewer tells us, is "*most strong, pointed,* and *specific.*" He puts it forward as if it were able of itself to sustain the doctrine of the resurrection of the same material body, to silence all the gainsayers in the New Church, and to cover them with shame and confusion. What now becomes of this passage? Why, of this very text, the present Bishop of London observes, "*I do not lay much stress* upon our Saviour's words, which are urged by Witsius, in proof of a resurrection of the same body, *the hour is coming, in the which all that are in the graves shall hear his voice!*" (Sermons, Notes.) How can this be, if the text is so strong, nay, further, most strong, and pointed? Yet the learned prelate will not lay much stress upon it! Why not? Another prelate, Bishop Newton, may perhaps explain the matter in the Dissertation already mentioned. (Vol. vi. p. 285.)

"In the New Testament, though the doctrine of the general resurrection is so much insisted upon, and such frequent mention is made of the resurrection of the dead, yet we nowhere read of the resurrection of the same body. Our Saviour saith, (John, v. 28,) 'All that are in the graves shall hear his voice and come forth,' and what are in the graves but the dead bodies? But if this is any proof of the resurrection of the body, it proveth too much, that the dead bodies can hear and come forth without their souls; for I presume it will hardly be said that the souls are in the graves too. It will also prove that the very same bodies, whether swollen with dropsies or wasted by consumptions, shall come forth in the same form and manner as they are laid in the graves. *All that are in the graves*, is nothing more than a periphrasis for the dead, they who have done good, and they who have done evil, which cannot possibly be applied to dead bodies."

So says Bishop Newton. Thus we have two eminent Bishops of the Church of England giving up this text as a proof of the resurrection of the same body; and yet the Reviewer continues to urge it, as if none but members of the New Church had ever thought of calling it in question as an authority for the resurrection of the same body; and as if they were consequently "profane and vain babblers, mischievous and destructive teachers." But is it not an awful state of the Church to find, upon this most solemn subject, one divine declaring the resurrection of the same body, as Witsius, to be the one grand hope and consolation of the Christian; another divine, as Bishop Pearson, declaring it to be a necessary and infallible truth; another divine, as Bishop Bull, resting upon it the whole doctrine of eternal happiness in heaven: and then to find other divines, equally eminent in learning and station, giving a flat contradiction to these statements, and challenging these theologians to prove that any such doctrine is to be found in the Bible? There are many, alas! who call themselves Christians, who give but little heed to these things, in consequence of going after the god of this world; but can you think that to those who desire to work out their salvation, this state of things in the Church is a matter of no consequence? Or can you wonder that it should have deeply affected many reflecting minds, and caused them to receive the doctrines of a New Church, in which they are satisfied there are no such contradictions; in which they perceive both certainty and clearness; and which, consequently, they regard as most consolatory?

"But," says the Reviewer, "the time when the resurrection is to take place is also marked out. It is to be when the trumpet shall sound, and when all who are found living upon earth shall be changed, as well as all the dead arise;" and the Reviewer says, "this cannot possibly agree with the notions of Swedenborg's disciples." I admit that they give quite another interpretation to the passage from the one commonly received. Hervey, and many other divines, describe the blast of the trumpet to be louder than ten thousand thunders, so very loud as to wake the dead; though it is difficult to conceive how those whose organs of hearing have to be formed, should be able to hear without them—how intensity of noise will compensate for utter insensibility to it. But not only is the noise assumed to be indescribably loud, but the dimensions of the instrument sounded are often conceived to be of proportionable extent. The Mahomedans believed, that because at the last day the deeds of men would be weighed in a balance, there would be an enormous pair of scales, stretching from over the regions of Paradise to the place over the regions of hell. But, as Mr. Sale observes, "some are willing to understand what is said in the Koran concerning this balance allegorically, and only as a figurative representation of God's equity; yet the more ancient and orthodox opinion is, that they are to be taken literally." In the present case, a most ancient and orthodox opinion is, that the trumpet is to be a literal trumpet; and in this case, well may Dr. Tilloch and other divines regard this literal rendering of the words as pure, unmixed nonsense. Here again, then, in the old Church, the inquiring Christian is baffled and put to a stand. He is told the trumpet shall sound. What trumpet? for the Apocalypse speaks of seven trumpets. St. Paul says, the last trumpet. According to commentators, six of the trumpets have sounded for a long time. Has the Reviewer, has any one else heard any of them? Besides, under this last trumpet, there are two resurrections, one described as taking place a thousand years before the other;—which of these resurrections does the Reviewer mean? When he says the time is distinctly marked out, we ask, which time? for there are two distinct times specified; with a difference of a thousand years between them. St Paul is universally admitted to refer only to the resurrection of the saints, the resurrection of the saints in the Apocalypse, is the first resurrection, and I know of scarcely a single commentator who agrees with the Reviewer in saying, that this is the time when *all* the dead shall arise. It is notorious that the whole subject is involved in inextricable difficulties. Still I acknowledge that a large number of divines, and with them Christians in general, have a very easy way of escaping, and that is, by putting aside the Apocalypse altogether. The Reviewer charges us with adding to the Word of God; but how can they who neglect the Apocalypse escape the charge of taking away from the Word of God? No man can read the explanations of the Apocalypse which have been published of late years, even by divines of the Church of England, without frequently meeting with charges against their own order of virtually taking away from the Word of God, in consequence of their leaving out the Apocalypse altogether, and hence being blind to the signs of the times—reckless of the warnings given to the Church—and crying peace, peace, when there is no peace.'

BIBLIOLIFE

Old Books Deserve a New Life
www.bibliolife.com

Did you know that you can get most of our titles in our trademark **EasyScript**™ print format? **EasyScript**™ provides readers with a larger than average typeface, for a reading experience that's easier on the eyes.

Did you know that we have an ever-growing collection of books in many languages?

Order online:
www.bibliolife.com/store

Or to exclusively browse our **EasyScript**™ collection:
www.bibliogrande.com

At BiblioLife, we aim to make knowledge more accessible by making thousands of titles available to you – quickly and affordably.

Contact us:
BiblioLife
PO Box 21206
Charleston, SC 29413